P9-CJU-939

Multi-Ethnic Literature

- ☐ Afro-American Authors
- ☐ American Indian Authors
- ☐ Asian-American Authors
- ☐ Mexican-American Authors
- ■ Chicano Voices

Chicano Voices

Carlota Cárdenas de Dwyer
Department of English
and Center for Mexican American Studies,
University of Texas at Austin

TINO VILLANUEVA, editorial adviser
Department of Spanish,
Wellesley College, Wellesley, Massachusetts

Houghton Mifflin Company • Boston
Atlanta Dallas Geneva, Ill. Hopewell, N.J. Palo Alto

Printed in the U.S.A.

Library of Congress Catalog Card Number: 75–13954

ISBN: 0–395–20579–4

ACKNOWLEDGMENTS

Leonard Adamé, "My Grandmother Would Rock Quietly and Hum" in *From the Barrio: A Chicano Anthology* by Luis Omar Salinas and Lillian Faderman. Copyright © 1973 by Luis Omar Salinas and Lillian Faderman. By permission of Harper & Row, Publishers, Inc.

Alurista, "address" and "when raza?" from *Floricanto en Aztlán* by Alurista. © Copyright 1971 by the Regents of the University of California. Reprinted by permission of the author.

Raymond Barrio, "Mi Vida" from *The Plum Plum Pickers.* © Copyright 1969 by Raymond Barrio and by Ventura Press. Reprinted by permission of the author.

Fabiola Cabeza de Baca, "The Women of New Mexico" from *We Fed Them Cactus* by Fabiola Cabeza de Baca. Copyright 1954 by the University of New Mexico Press.

Jaime Darío Calvillo, "The White Milkman" from *Tejidos: A Bilingual Journal for the Stimulation of Chicano Creativity & Criticism,* Spring 1974. Copyright © 1974 by Tejidos. Reprinted by permission of the author.

Fray Angélico Chávez, "Rattlesnake," copyright 1945. Reprinted by permission of the author.

César Chávez, "The Organizer's Tale" from *Ramparts,* July 1966. Copyright © 1966 by *Ramparts.*

Marta Cotera, "When Women Speak" from *Event,* January 1974 (revised from an article originally published in *Magazín, La Revista del Mejicano de Tejas,* September 1973). Copyright © 1973, 1974. Reprinted by permission of the author.

Abelardo Delgado, "stupid america" from *Chicano: 25 Pieces of a Chicano Mind* by Abelardo, Barrio Publications, 1972. Reprinted by permission of the author.

Ernesto Galarza, "On the Edge of the Barrio" from *Barrio Boy.* Copyright © 1971 by University of Notre Dame Press.

Rodolfo Gonzales, "I Am Joaquín" from *I Am Joaquín.* Copyright © 1967 by Rodolfo Gonzales. Reprinted by permission of the author.

Rolando R. Hinojosa-S., "The Maestro" and "My Aunt Panchita" from *Estampas del Valle y Otras Obras/Sketches of the Valley and Other Works,* Quinto Sol Publications, Inc. Copyright 1973 by Rolando R. Hinojosa-S. Reprinted by permission.

Enriqueta Longeaux y Vásquez, "The Woman of La Raza" from *Sisterhood Is Powerful* edited by Robin Morgan, Vintage Books. Copyright © 1970 by Enriqueta Longeaux y Vásquez. Reprinted by permission of the author.

Enrique Hank López, "Overkill at the Silver Dollar" from *The Nation,* October 19, 1970. Copyright 1970 in the U.S.A. by the Nation Associates, Inc.

George Meneses, "Chavalo Encanicado" from *Con Safos,* Winter 1971. Copyright © Con Safos, Inc., 1971. Reprinted by permission.

Philip D. Ortego, "Between Two Cultures" from "Schools for Mexican-Americans: Between Two Cultures" by Philip D. Ortego in *Saturday Review,* April 17, 1971. © 1971 by Saturday Review, Inc. Used by permission of the magazine.

Américo Paredes, "The Hammon and the Beans" from *The Texas Observer,* April 18, 1963. Copyright © 1963 by The Texas Observer Company, Ltd. Reprinted by permission of the author.

Leroy Quintana, "piñones" from *New Mexico Magazine,* November/December 1974. Copyright © 1974. Reprinted by permission of the author.

John Rechy, "El Paso del Norte," from *Evergreen Review,* Autumn 1958. Copyright 1958 by Evergreen Review, Inc. Reprinted by permission of Harold Matson Company.

Tomás Rivera, "The Prayer" and "When We Arrive" (slightly abridged) from *". . . y no se lo tragó la tierra"/". . . and the earth did not part."* Copyright 1971 by Quinto Sol Publications, Inc. Reprinted by permission.

Floyd Salas, "Dead Time" from *Tattoo the Wicked Cross,* reprinted by permission of Grove Press, Inc. Copyright © 1967 by Floyd Salas.

Rubén Salazar, "Stranger in One's Land" from *Stranger in One's Land,* U.S. Commission on Civil Rights Clearinghouse Publication No. 19, May 1970.

Raúl Salinas first presented "sinfonía serrana," copyright © 1975 by raúlrsalinas, at the 1974 Festival de Flor y Canto at the University of Southern California. Reprinted with his permission.

Danny Santiago, "The Somebody," first published in *Redbook.* Copyright © 1970 by Danny Santiago. Reprinted by permission of Brandt & Brandt.

Sabine Ulibarrí, "The Stuffing of the Lord" from *Tierra Amarilla* by Sabine Ulibarrí, translated by Thelma Campbell Nason. Copyright 1971 by the University of New Mexico Press.

Luis Valdez, *Los Vendidos* from *Actos: El Teatro Campesino.* © 1971 Cucaracha Publications/El Centro Campesino Cultural. Reprinted by permission.

Richard Vásquez, "Angelina Sandoval" from *Chicano.* Copyright © 1970 by Richard Vásquez. Reprinted by permission of Doubleday & Co., Inc.

Tino Villanueva, "Day-Long Day" and "Pachuco Remembered" from *Hay Otra Voz Poems* by Tino Villanueva, Colección Mensaje, 1972. Reprinted by permission of the author.

José Antonio Villarreal, "The World of Richard Rubio" from *Pocho.* Copyright © 1959 by José Antonio Villarreal. Reprinted by permission of Doubleday & Co., Inc.

Edmund Villaseñor, "The Compadre" and "The Sánchez Sisters" from *Macho!* by Edmund Villaseñor. Copyright © 1973 by Edmund Victor Villaseñor. Published by Bantam Books, Inc. All rights reserved.

Introduction

The Chicano voices of this collection articulate various aspects of what has come to be known as the Chicano experience. No single theme can encompass all that Chicanos have experienced since our indigenous ancestors traveled over all of the Americas or since our Hispanic ancestors first explored the Southwest in the sixteenth century. However, although Chicano life today extends over a spectrum as extensive as our historical past, some incidents are so common that they may be thought of as forming a shared Chicano experience.

Some of these experiences, like the memories that Leonard Adamé describes in "My Grandmother Would Rock Quietly and Hum," are beautiful and private. Other experiences, like those in Sabine Ulibarrí's "The Stuffing of the Lord," are recounted in a way that is humorous and lighthearted. Still others, like those of Américo Paredes' "The Hammon and the Beans" and Enrique Hank López's "Overkill at the Silver Dollar," are tragic and disturbing. Whatever its subject or theme, each of the voices heard here tells a story which is best understood and appreciated within the framework of the history of the Mexican American people in the United States.

To Chicanos, the Fifth of May is as familiar as the Fourth of July, and the Treaty of Guadalupe-Hidalgo is as significant as the Declaration of Independence. Living on the frontiers of two dynamic civilizations, Chicanos have witnessed the evolution of two great societies and from them have created a distinct Chicano culture. The Chicano heritage is a blend of all that has come before.

This anthology emphasizes the contemporary, although it represents three generations. As of this writing, all the authors except Rubén Salazar are living; many are young. Along with several newer writers, most of the major

Chicano authors are represented in this collection. Fortunately, in only a few cases was it not possible to make the necessary arrangements for reprinting selections that were intended for inclusion in the anthology.

Just as the major writers have been gathered here, so too are the important themes of Chicano literature, which have provided an organization for the anthology. The collection could have been arranged in many other ways. Writers might have been grouped to represent the different states of the Southwest, sometimes referred to as Aztlán. California writers — Luis Valdez, Ernesto Galarza, and others — might have been distinguished from such New Mexico writers as Leroy Quintana, Fabiola Cabeza de Baca, and Father Chávez, and from such Texas writers as Rolando Hinojosa-S., Jaime Darío Calvillo, and Ricardo Sánchez. Women writers — of whom there are still too few — might have been separated from men, or prose writers from poets. A strictly chronological order of selections might have been followed. The possibilities are numerous.

Each unit of the anthology exemplifies what the text as a whole seeks to accomplish. That is, individually and collectively the units offer a representative variety of writers, genres, and views. The themes chosen not only are related but seem sometimes to contain one another. The Chicano people of the first unit often live in The Barrio of the second unit. The relationship of a selection and a unit theme may be as direct as the connection of César Chávez's narrative with La Causa, the subject of the fifth unit, or as indirect as that of Abelardo's poem in the same unit. Thus it is not surprising that several male authors should be included in the unit about The Chicana. The hushed voice created by Tomás Rivera in "A Prayer" is as authentic and representative as Marta Cotera's outspoken words in her essay "When Women Speak" or as Enriqueta Vásquez's in "The Woman of La Raza." Like the subtle hues and vibrant colors of a Chicano mural, the blending together of the different voices in this collection re-creates the experience of an entire people.

The question of language — or, more accurately, languages — is of the greatest significance in the understanding of Chicano literature. For many Chicanos, Spanish and

English are equally useful in communication. Sometimes it is more appropriate and emphatic to use one Spanish word rather than three English words, as when Alurista says "ahorita" instead of "this very moment." Sometimes there are other, more complex, considerations. The language of this anthology includes Chicano Spanish expressions that are an intrinsic part of the Chicano identity and experience. Because Spanish and English are joined in the actual speech of Chicanos, one language has not been differentiated from the other in print through the use of italics.

Because understanding is a basis for appreciation, however, English translations of Spanish words have been supplied for the reader who needs them. Since creative writing is by nature the careful and artistic use of language, and of languages, even the best translations must be regarded as approximations. The subtle associations and shades of meaning so crucial to the fullest appreciation of a poem or story are often blurred in translation. The greatest difficulties in translation seem to occur with words that describe people. When George Meneses describes a minor character as "chiple," he does not simply mean "pampered." The word has other connotations which are lost in translation. Sometimes, even when an apposite meaning is found, as when one translates *mujer* as "woman," the resulting changes in aspiration and sound are so different as to affect the character of the meaning. When dealing with literature, one can never forget that language is infinitely complex, that translations can be a guide only to a surface level of communication.

Looking closely at the literature in this collection, one might say that each writer here has created his or her own language. None could be mistaken for another. All have developed their idiom from their experiences, their education, and their choices. Writers make words work for them. The challenge to the reader is to hear and respond to all that is created. It is hoped that the Chicano writers of this collection will serve as a stimulus to further reading in the area of Chicano literature.

The word *Chicano* is used here as it is used by most of the writers themselves: as a label of ethnic identity and pride.

Contents

La Raza/The Chicano People

El Barrio/The Barrio

La Chicana/The Chicana Woman

La Vida/Life

La Causa/The Chicano Movement

Illustrations

Chicano Voices

La Raza

The Chicano People

I withdraw to the safety within the
circle of life —

MY OWN PEOPLE.

Rodolfo Gonzales

ARTURO
ROMAN

ALURISTA

address

Born in Mexico but raised in California, Alurista is a leading Chicano poet. His work reveals a concern with both the Indian and the Spanish cultures that form the Chicano heritage, as well as his view of the modern culture in which Chicanos live. In "address," for example, the reader finds not just two different languages — the English of an application form and the Spanish words of a Chicano encountering it — but the contrasting values of two different worlds.

address
occupation
age
marital status
— perdone . . .
        yo me llamo pedro[1]
telephone
height
hobbies
previous employers
— perdone . . .
        yo me llamo pedro[1]
        pedro ortega
zip code
i.d. number
classification
rank
— perdone mi padre era
        el señor ortega
        (a veces don josé)[2]
race

1 *perdone . . . pedro* pardon/my name is Pedro. 2 *perdone . . . (a veces don josé)* pardon, my father was/señor Ortega/(sometimes called don José)

Américo Paredes

The Hammon and the Beans

In this short story the narrator recalls Chonita, an acquaintance of his youth. Although there were many differences between himself and Chonita, he seemed to accept the brave young girl in a way that none of the other children did. Américo Paredes' story is notable for its sensitive portrayal of a Mexican American child's first inklings of the conflict between his own background and the culture in which he lives. Dr. Paredes, who is best known as the author of With His Pistol in His Hand *and other collections of folklore, was born and raised in Brownsville, Texas — a city that in many ways resembles the Jonesville-on-the-Grande of the story.*

Once we lived in one of my grandfather's houses near Fort Jones. It was just a block from the parade grounds, a big frame house painted a dirty yellow. My mother hated it, especially because of the pigeons that cooed all day about the eaves. They had fleas, she said. But it was a quiet neighborhood at least, too far from the center of town for automobiles and too near for musical, night-roaming drunks.

At this time Jonesville-on-the-Grande was not the thriving little city that it is today. We told off our days by the routine on the post. At six sharp the flag was raised on the parade grounds to the cackling of the bugles, and a field piece thundered out a salute. The sound of the shot bounced away through the morning mist until its echoes worked their way into every corner of town. Jonesville-on-the-Grande woke to the cannon's roar, as if to battle, and the day began.

At eight the whistle from the post laundry sent us children off to school. The whole town stopped for lunch with the noon whistle, and after lunch everybody went back to work when the post laundry said that it was one o'clock, except for those who could afford to be old-fashioned and took the siesta. The post was the town's clock, you might have said, or like some insistent elder person who was always there to tell you it was time.

At six the flag came down, and we went to watch through the high wire fence that divided the post from the town. Sometimes we joined in the ceremony, standing at salute until the sound of the cannon made us jump. That must have been when we had just studied about George Washington in school, or recited "The Song of Marion's Men," about Marion the Fox and the British cavalry that chased him up and down the broad Santee. But at other times we stuck out our tongues and jeered at the soldiers. Perhaps the night before, we had hung at the edges of a group of old men and listened to tales about Aniceto Pizaña[1] and the "border troubles," as the local paper still called them when it referred to them gingerly in passing.

It was because of the border troubles, ten years or so before, that the soldiers had come back to old Fort Jones. But we did not hate them for that; we admired them, even, at least sometimes. But when we were thinking about the border troubles instead of Marion the Fox, we hooted them and the flag they were lowering, which for the moment was theirs alone, just as we would have jeered an opposing ball team, in a friendly sort of way. On these occasions even Chonita would join in the mockery, though she usually ran home at the stroke of six. But whether we taunted or saluted, the distant men in khaki uniforms went about their motions without noticing us at all.

The last word from the post came in the night when a distant bugle blew. At nine it was all right because all the lights were on. But sometimes I heard it at eleven, when everything was dark and still, and it made me feel that I was all alone in the world. I would even doubt that I was me, and that put me in such a fright that I felt like yelling out just to make sure I was really there. But next

1 *Aniceto Pizaña* leader of a guerrilla group that urged the separation of the southern part of Texas from the Union about 1915

morning the sun shone and life began all over again, with its whistles and cannon shots and bugles blowing. And so we lived, we and the post, side by side with the wire fence in between.

The wandering soldiers whom the bugle called home at night did not wander in our neighborhood, and none of us ever went into Fort Jones. None except Chonita. Every evening when the flag came down, she would leave off playing and go down towards what was known as the "lower" gate of the post, the one that opened not on Main Street but against the poorest part of town. She went into the grounds and to the mess halls and pressed her nose against the screens and watched the soldiers eat. They sat at long tables, calling to each other through food-stuffed mouths.

"Hey, bud, pass the coffee!"

"Give me the ham!"

"Yeah, give me the beans!"

After the soldiers were through, the cooks came out and scolded Chonita, and then they gave her packages with things to eat.

Chonita's mother did our washing, in gratefulness — as my mother put it — for the use of a vacant lot of my grandfather's which was a couple of blocks down the street. On the lot was an old one-room shack which had been a shed long ago, and this Chonita's father had patched up with flattened-out pieces of tin. He was a laborer. Ever since the end of the border troubles there had been a development boom in the Valley, and Chonita's father was getting his share of the good times. Clearing brush and building irrigation ditches, he sometimes pulled down as much as six dollars a week. He drank a good deal of it up, it was true. But corn was just a few cents a bushel in those days. He was the breadwinner, you might say, while Chonita furnished the luxuries.

Chonita was a poet, too. I had just moved into the neighborhood when a boy came up to me and said, "Come on! Let's go hear Chonita make a speech."

She was already on top of the alley fence when we got there, a scrawny little girl of about nine, her bare dirty feet clinging to the fence almost like hands. A dozen other kids were there below her, waiting. Some were boys I knew at school; five or six were her younger brothers and sisters.

"Speech! Speech!" they all cried. "Let Chonita make a speech! Talk in English, Chonita!"

They were grinning and nudging each other, except for her brothers and sisters, who looked up at her with proud, serious faces. She gazed out beyond us all with a grand, distant air and then she spoke.

"Give me the hammon and the beans!" she yelled. "Give me the hammon and the beans!"

She leaped off the fence, and everybody cheered and told her how good it was and how she could talk English better than the teachers at the grammar school.

I thought it was a pretty poor joke. Every evening almost, they would make her get up on the fence and yell, "Give me the hammon and the beans!" And everybody would cheer and make her think she was talking English. As for me, I would wait there until she got it over with, so we could play at something else. I wondered how long it would be before they got tired of it all. I never did find out, because just about that time I got the chills and fever, and when I got up and around Chonita wasn't there anymore.

In later years I thought of her a lot, especially during the thirties, when I was growing up. Those years would have been just made for her. Many's the time I have seen her in my mind's eyes, in the picket lines demanding not bread, not cake, but the hammon and the beans. But it didn't work out that way.

One night Dr. Zapata came into our kitchen through the back door. He set his bag on the table and said to my father, who had opened the door for him, "Well, she is dead."

My father flinched. "What was it?" he asked.

The doctor had gone to the window and he stood with his back to us, looking out toward the light of Fort Jones. "Pneumonia, flu, malnutrition, worms, the evil eye," he said without turning around. "What the hell difference does it make?"

"I wish I had known how sick she was," my father

said in a very mild tone. "Not that it's really my affair, but I wish I had."

The doctor snorted and shook his head.

My mother came in and I asked her who was dead. She told me. It made me feel strange but I did not cry. My mother put her arm around my shoulders. "She is in Heaven now," she said. "She is happy."

I shrugged her arm away and sat down in one of the kitchen chairs.

"They're like animals," the doctor was saying. He turned round suddenly and his eyes glistened in the light. "Do you know what that brute of a father was doing when I left? He was laughing! Drinking and laughing with his friends."

"There's no telling what the poor man feels," my mother said.

My father made a deprecatory gesture. "It wasn't his daughter anyway."

"No?" the doctor said. He sounded interested.

"This is the woman's second husband," my father explained. "First one died before the girl was born — shot and hanged from a mesquite limb. He was working too close to the tracks the day the Olmito train was derailed." [2]

"You know what?" the doctor said. "In classical times they did things better. Take Troy, for instance. After they stormed the city, they grabbed the babies by the heels and dashed them against the wall. That was more humane."

My father smiled. "You sound very radical. You sound just like your relative down there in Morelos." [3]

"No relative of mine," the doctor said. "I'm a conservative, the son of a conservative, and you know that I wouldn't be here except for that little detail."

"Habit," my father said. "Pure habit, pure tradition. You're a radical at heart."

"It depends on how you define radicalism," the doc-

2 *"First one . . . train was derailed."* probably a reference to the reprisals for the activities of Pizaña's guerrillas

3 *your relative . . . Morelos* a reference to Emiliano Zapata, from the state of Morelos, who led revolutionary forces against the Mexican government early in the second decade of the 1900s

tor answered. "People tend to use words too loosely. A dentist *could* be called a radical, I suppose. He pulls up things by the roots."

My father chuckled.

"Any bandit in Mexico nowadays can give himself a political label," the doctor went on, "and that makes him respectable. He's a leader of the people."

"Take Villa,[4] now — " my father began.

"Villa was a different type of man," the doctor broke in.

"I don't see any difference."

The doctor came over to the table and sat down. "Now look at it this way," he began, his finger in front of my father's face. My father threw back his head and laughed.

"You'd better go to bed and rest," my mother told me. "You're not completely well, you know."

So I went to bed, but I didn't go to sleep, not right away. I lay there for a long time while behind my darkened eyelids Emiliano Zapata's cavalry charged down to the broad Santee, where there were grave men with hoary hairs. I was still awake at eleven, when the cold voice of the bugle went gliding in and out of the dark like something that couldn't find its way back to wherever it had been. I thought of Chonita in Heaven, and I saw her in her torn and dirty dress, with a pair of bright wings attached, flying round and round like a butterfly, shouting, "Give me the hammon and the beans!"

Then I cried. And whether it was the bugle, or whether it was Chonita or what, to this day I do not know. But cry I did, and I felt much better after that.

4 *Villa* Mexican revolutionist and contemporary of Zapata

ROLANDO R. HINOJOSA-S.

The Maestro

This portrait is from a collection of sketches that portray life in the Rio Grande Valley of south Texas, where the author has spent much of his life. The Valley people he recalls come to life through accounts by such characters as Rafa (Rafael), bartender at the Aquí Me Quedo ("Here I Shall Stay"), who tells here about don Genaro Castañeda, "el Maistro." The word maistro *is a colloquial form of* maestro, *which means master craftsman.*

Lucas Barrón, the owner of the tavern Aquí Me Quedo, is called "el Chorreao." [1]

"Because he never takes a bath?"

"Exactly."

El Chorreao has many customers and, among them, a very special one: "el Maistro" (Maestro), don Genaro Castañeda. El Maistro is a housepainter and once, many years ago, the government called him to arms: to lend his services for the defense of the nation against its enemies and for Liberty, etc., etc., etc.

That was the First World War and so they took el Maistro away. First to San Antonio for the physical exam, then to another military base the location of which he never found out. Finally they arrived at New York Harbor and then crossed the ocean to France, where the war was being fought then.

According to el Maistro, it wasn't so bad. He spoke a little English, he ate what there was, and they paid him almost every month, although he didn't know where to spend it. He recalls that on one occasion, when he was in the trench, he was hit by a piece of shrapnel the size of a

1 *"el Chorreao"* "Grubby" or "Grimy" (a nickname)

BB. When he felt the sting, he put his hand to his forehead and saw the little ball. He says that he kept on looking at it for a little while and since nothing happened to him, he let it fall in a puddle of water close to where he was standing guard. He got a rather nasty scratch from barbed wire and that's how he shed a few drops of blood on French soil.

When the shooting stopped, he was put on another ship, crossed the ocean again, and then was taken back to San Antonio by train. There he was given more money and then dispatched by bus to Klail, which he's never left since.

As time went on, el Maistro got married and, with the assistance of his wife, had a horde of children. As he says, some are smart and some are dumb, but they all eat.

A peaceful man, el Maistro, like many painters, is a great drinker of beer, whiskey, wine, and whatever else is in sight. It must be the fate of the profession — who knows? — but that's how it is and that's that.

El Maistro must be at least seventy-five years old but he still paints and, to tell the truth, he still has a drink or two or whatever his liver can take. With his two friends, Echevarría and Leal, who are more or less of the same age, el Maistro talks about those things that old men in Klail and the world over, for that matter, always discuss.

By chance I found out that he was a veteran of the First World War, but I don't pester him with questions although I enjoy his conversation. I was in the Korean War for quite a while and, although I am a young man, it seems to me that el Maistro and I shared almost identical experiences: they passed like clouds that are dispersed by air and time.

The American Legion post in Klail is new since the Second World War and the name on the door is that of Pfc. Joseph T. Hargan, who died in '43 in Salerno. The members of the Chamber of Commerce, the Rotarians, the Lions, and interested or just anxious citizens — none of them are aware that el Maistro is a veteran of the First World War. Perhaps they just don't care. . . .

Here comes el Maistro.

"What can I do for you, don Genaro?"

"A coupla beers, Rafa: a Pearl for me and one for Echevarría and a Jax for Leal."

"Okay, don Genaro. I'll bring them to your booth."

"Thanks, son."

El Maistro goes back to his table where his two friends are waiting, and I pick out the coldest beer.

EDMUND VILLASEÑOR

The Compadre

This chapter from the novel Macho! *by the California writer Edmund Villaseñor is set in a remote Mexican village of the 1960s. In the chapter and throughout the novel Villaseñor explores the traditional rules of behavior and respect, as well as the ways in which traditions are being challenged. This chapter concerns a special relationship in Mexican and Mexican American culture: that of compadres. Villaseñor explains the relationship in this way: "When you and your woman, or a close relative if you are not married, baptize another couple's child in the Holy Catholic Church, you then become not only the child's godparents, but you, as a man, become the other man's dearest friend, his compadre."*

It was late at night when Roberto got home, and he was hungry and tired and barely had the energy to put the horse up before going under the lean-to to eat. Getting there, he found his compadre. And his mother said, "Your compadre, a wonderful man, has been waiting for you so you can eat dinner together."

"Oh," said Roberto, seeing that his compadre had brought along his two biggest children, and not the little one he had baptized a few months back. "Have you been waiting long, compadre?"

"Oh," said his compadre, "not too long. I have been here waiting for you, my compadre, only since the sun set. That is all. I don't mind."

"Oh," said Roberto as he washed his hands and sat down on the log bench by the warmth of the fire. "I am glad you don't mind."

"No. Of course not. We are compadres!"

"Yes. We are. Tell me . . . how are you passing it? Ah, how are you passing these days?"

"Well," he said, and shrugged. "You know how it is with the crops. Bad. And there is no work now that we got our own personal crop in."

"Work? I can use another plower of bueyes." [1]

"Bueyes? Oh, no thank you, compadre. I am not so good with them and the sun. I get sick out in those treeless fields."

"Oh. I see. Tell me . . . have you and your children had dinner?"

"Why, no, compadre. Of course not! That would have been rude. Your kind, wonderful, and most gracious mother invited me to join her and the family, but I declined. I wished to wait for you!"

"Oh," said Roberto. "That is very thoughtful of you."

His mother was now bringing plates of barbecue and frijoles and a bundle of tortillas. She set these on the two old wooden crates that had the faded imprint of Cutty Sark scotch and a sailing ship. Where Roberto's father had found these boxes, no one knew. But they were good boxes for eating from, and they, the family, felt proud to own such boxes with a sailing ship. They figured fish had come in these wood boxes. Fish from the sea that was supposedly over there. That way. Far far away.

Roberto nodded and begged for his compadre to start first and watched, taking note of how much his compadre served himself; and then he, Roberto, began, and he said, "Mama? This is a lot of barbecue. Did you not eat some yourself?"

She grew nervous and said, "Yes! Of course!"

"No, she didn't!" said one of Roberto's smallest brothers. "We had none. She saved it all for you."

Roberto froze in half-stride to feed his mouth. He glanced at his mother. She was all nerves. He glanced at his compadre and saw how he kept eating and quickly feeding his two kids and acting as though he had not heard. Roberto said nothing; then, after a while, he got up and handed his plate of food to his little brother and saw how he and three others came to it like hungry little dogs,

1 *bueyes* oxen

and he said, "Compadre . . . my dearest compadre!"

"Yes?"

"You came to eat with me yesterday. Did you not?"

"Well . . . I came to visit, and it happened that . . . you know . . . yourself, invited me to your most gracious table."

"It happened, ah? Just happened that you arrived at about dinnertime. Well, *listen,* my dearest compadre.

"Tonight, eat! I can see that you and your children are hungry. So eat! Enjoy our food! And I feel good and honored to have you as a guest *but,* unless you show up for work tomorrow morning and start inviting me to *your table* — " And on these last two words his voice thickened and his eyes narrowed small and mad and his jaw muscles quivered. "Never come here again and just *happen* to get invited to our table." He stopped. He breathed and added, "I speak clearly, do I not?"

"Yes. You speak clearly . . . and . . . and for one being so young and being a compadre! God forbid! I'll attend the church for you tomorrow. I'll . . . I'll — " And he stopped talking, ate quickly, finished his plate, and got up. "Come, children. Finish up and let us go!" And he, the compadre for life in the Holy Catholic Church, left in a big hurry. "Never will I shadow your path as long as I breathe!"

"Good!" yelled Roberto. "Good!"

And Roberto's mother began scolding him, telling him that the rumors were true. Were true! He indeed had lost all respect and sold his soul to el diablo,[2] and that was why he was doing so well, and one thousand times one thousand she would rather have them poor and hungry than to have him, her firstborn, condemned to hell forever and ever. His father, big Roberto, would hear of this. He would know what to do with a muchacho[3] who talked disrespectfully to his elders and . . . my God! a COMPADRE on top of that! And she began to pray, and Roberto ignored her and watched his young brothers and sisters eat,

2 *el diablo* the devil
3 *muchacho* boy

and he turned, saying that he was going to the plaza, to the center of the pueblo, to see about some business.

She, his mother, old and squat, and yet not even thirty-three years old, called, "Please . . . don't go! Please! Oh, my God! What have we done wrong, my Lord God." And she told her eldest daughter to run after him. "For the sake of God!"

The oldest daughter ran out to the street and caught her brother. "Roberto?"

He heard his sister's voice, and he stopped. "Yes." If it had been anyone else he would have kept going, but Esperanza, meaning Hope, was different from most girls. She had argued her way out of the house, out of the traditional job of the eldest daughter being like a second mother to all the younger children, and she had gone to school. Which was fantastic. For no eldest daughter in the village had ever done so. "What do you want?"

"Nothing. I just came to say you did the right thing. That damn freeloader!" And she raised her hand in a fist. "If I were a man, I would have hit him!"

Roberto smiled. His sister was thin and dark and had huge brown eyes, and when she used words like *damn* her face became so strong and righteous that he couldn't think of her as a girl. She was so different from other girls. She was smart and quick, and he liked her as a person, a friend, someone to talk to. Almost like another man.

"Thank you," he said. "Thank you. Now, go on home. Take care of Mama. I have business."

"With the norteños?" [4]

He eyed her. "How'd you know?"

She shrugged. "How do we know anything in this small town?"

He looked at his sister, and there she stood, dark and arrogant, and he knew what she meant. She read books, and she was always complaining about this being a small town. Always. As long as he could recall. He nodded. Her reading seemed to do nothing but make her more and more

4 *norteños* men who travel north to work in the United States

unhappy. But he said nothing. They had argued about this before, and it had never helped. She was a dreamer. She was always confusing her mind with faraway things and forgetting the immediate. He nodded. He patted her on the head.

"Yes. I go to see the norteños. But don't worry . . . I won't go north."

"Why not? If I were a man . . . hell, I would have left this lousy place years ago!"

He stiffened. "Esperanza, I forbid you to talk this way. God made you a woman. He had his reasons. You are not to question. Have respect! Is it not bad enough that I broke customs tonight? Ah! Is not once enough?"

She smiled, and her eyes went large and brown and full of fun and mischief. "If I were a man," she repeated, "I'd break all the customs every day!"

Roberto began to speak, to anger, but then stopped . . . and held. Saying nothing. His sister was so ungirllike. It was hopeless. Boys didn't even call on her because of her infamous sharp tongue.

She smiled and took his hand and spoke as if she knew his thoughts. "Don't worry about me. I just talk tough to you. After all, you're the only one I can talk to." She blew him a kiss and turned, running down the rock-laid street in large graceful bounds.

He watched until she was within their jacal;[5] then he turned, going into the night. Poor thing . . . she was hopeless. She would never get a husband the way she behaved. Never. She was already sixteen and still single.

5 *jacal* shanty; shack

JAIME DARÍO CALVILLO

The White Milkman

Out of his own experiences in south Texas the poet Jaime Darío Calvillo writes of Chicano life — here, of the contrast between past and present. In this poem he presents a woman absorbed in her memories. As she watches a milkman making his rounds, Mrs. Martínez recalls the lechero, or milk vendor, of her girlhood in Mexico. Shifting from present to past and back again, the poem brings all three characters into sharp focus.

Señora Martínez awaits an albino milkman.

In the morning when he comes
The sun is rising from the wire fence
and she cracks the door to let in the light.

Images of wax cartons se cuajan
a un lechero[1] hauling raw-milk tins on his cart.
Fat milk pours from silver tins to her pans.
"Esta leche va muy bien con pan dulce
por la mañana, señorita." [2]

The albino milkman's milk
comes cold
comes waxed
goes quickly to the icebox.

She sees the milkman.
The cartons dangle in his monstrous hands.
As he comes, his hair blazes brilliant white,
his speckled face sours in the light.

1 *Images . . . lechero* Images of wax cartons curdle/into (a vision of) a milk vendor. 2 *"Esta . . . señorita."* "This milk goes well with sweet bread/in the morning, señorita."

Señora Martínez quietly closes the door.

Behind the door el lechero has given leche bronca[3]
and, leaving, greets the day, "¡Leeeeeeche!
¡Leeeeeeeche fresca! [4]
Leeeeeeeeeche de cabra y vaca[5] . . . Leeeeeeche,
Leeeeeeche fresca. . . ."

3 *leche bronca* raw milk. 4 *fresca* fresh. 5 *de cabra y vaca* goat and cow's (milk)

Philip D. Ortego

Between Two Cultures

A professor of English who has taught at several universities, Philip D. Ortego currently acts as editor of La Luz *magazine. He has written short stories and poems as well as numerous articles, many of them about Chicano literature or about the social conditions of the Chicano. Published in 1971, this article is based upon an earlier treatment of the same subject. Although it should be read in the context of 1970, the article contains much information that is just as relevant today. As an educator, Dr. Ortego focuses on the place of the Chicano student in the American school system.*

They were here before the Conquistadores, before the Puritans, before the Pennsylvania Dutch, before the Irish of Boston or the Italians of New York or the Poles of Chicago. Despite the overlay of Spanish culture, Mexican Americans are essentially descendants of the great Mayan and Aztec civilizations, the children of Moctezuma. The face of Mexico even today is an Indian face. The pyramids of Teotihuacán seem more impressive than the elegant facade of Chapultepec Castle. The legend of Ixtacíhuatl fascinates more than do the exploits of Cortés. Although Spanish influences are everywhere visible in Mexico, it is the Indian character of the people that is more obvious. Yet, only in recent years has Indian blood rather than Spanish blood become a source of national Mexican pride. To be a Mexican today is to be a member of La Raza, the race of Moctezuma's children.

Yet, within the boundaries of the United States, Mexican Americans are still struggling to overcome not only the linguistic disadvantage of speaking a foreign language but the disadvantage of visibility — of looking like a

Mexican. In the Southwest — Texas, New Mexico, Colorado, Arizona, and California — where approximately eight million Chicanos live, they subsist on levels of survival exceedingly below national norms. Eighty percent live in predominantly urban environments, ranging from the megalopolis of Los Angeles — where more than a fifth of the Mexican Americans reside — to such small urban centers as Las Cruces, New Mexico, with a population of about 55,000, half of whom are Mexican Americans. Throughout the region they suffer the ills of discrimination in education, housing, and employment — ills that established the patterns of poverty of the barrios and colonias, the Mexican ghettos of the Southwest. Few non-Southwesterners realize, for instance, that brown Americans, like black Americans, were segregated in the schools in California until 1947 and in Texas schools until 1948.

This prejudice, this discrimination, many Mexican Americans argue, stems from the 1848 Treaty of Guadalupe-Hidalgo, a treaty that identified those who came with the conquered lands of the Southwest as a defeated people, a treaty that usurped their territorial rights and turned them into strangers in their own land. Those who came later, in the great migration of the early 1900s, have been equally victimized by the stereotypes engendered by the Mexican American War.

The consequence in recent years has been the formation of the Alianza in New Mexico led by the fiery Reies López Tijerina, who — though he may never succeed in his quixotic mission to recover the lands for the present claimants — nevertheless has elevated the social and political consciousness of many Mexican Americans to the point of demanding reformation of the socio-economic structure that has kept them subordinated these many years. In California, César Chávez has mobilized the grape pickers; and in Colorado, Corky Gonzales has infused the Mexican Americans with the spirit of protest.

Nevertheless, at the moment what continues to characterize Mexican Americans in the Southwest is the fact that most of them have a limited and inadequate education. The educational statistics on Mexican Americans are shocking. Their dropout rate is more than two times the national average, and estimates of the average number of school years completed by Mexican Americans (7.1 years) are significantly below figures for black children (9.0 years) or Anglo children (12.1 years). In Texas 39 percent of the Mexican Americans have less than a fifth-grade education, and Mexican Americans twenty-five years of age or older have as little as 4.8 years of schooling. Almost half of the Chicanos in Texas essentially are still functional illiterates.

In fact, many Mexican American youngsters never get to the first grade. In Texas only about one-third of the five- and six-year-old Chicanos are enrolled in school, and of those, four out of five fall two grades behind their Anglo classmates by the time they reach fifth grade. In California more than 50 percent of Mexican American high school students drop out between grades ten and eleven. Less than half of 1 percent of the college students enrolled on the seven campuses of the University of California are Mexican Americans, although they constitute more than 14 percent of the public school population of the state.

The high dropout rate cannot be blamed on a lack of emphasis on education in the home. A 1968 study by James Anderson and Dwight Johnson points out that "there appears to be little difference between Mexican American families and other families with respect to the amount of emphasis on education that the child experiences in his home." Moreover, "these children experience the same high degree of encouragement and assistance at home as do their classmates." The inescapable conclusion is that the academic failures of many Mexican American youngsters are the result of inadequate school programs rather than the consequence of low achievement or aspiration levels of their families.

The issues in Mexican American education are formidable, but they have thus far been approached simplistically. To begin with, existing education programs (with the exception of pilot or experimental model programs) make no allowance for the fact that many Mexican American children come to school either (a) knowing a fair amount of English but being psychologically reluctant to use it, (b) knowing little English, or else (c) knowing only Spanish. Thus, from the start, Chicano children are burdened with the disadvantage of being unable to deal with the national language. In many states English is prescribed by law as the official language of instruction, and Mexican American students are expressly forbidden to speak Spanish on the rationale that by speaking English the student will learn English.

Traditionally these children are herded into schools where the proceedings are conducted in a language they don't understand, via which they are expected to learn all the standard subjects, including reading. Usually their teachers are Anglo Americans who are not bilingual and who therefore cannot communicate to their charges the learning content of first grade. First grade, then, can become a traumatic experience in which the teacher, with little or no facility in Spanish and untrained in language theory and analysis, attempts to create enough English fluency in the pupils to begin the required instructional materials.

Just as this "come and get it" approach to the common curriculum fails to deal with the fundamental educational problems of Mexican Americans, so too does the more recent approach of preparing the child before he must enter school. Projects such as Head Start, Follow Through, and other preschool compensatory educational programs suffer from the assumption that all Spanish-speaking preschoolers who are recipients of such programs — short- or long-term, well-designed or inefficient — will be fluent in English and able to deal with a traditional curriculum. Six months of preschool alone is hardly enough time to overcome the disadvantage.

Thus, Mexican American children arrive at the schoolhouse door with educational needs their Anglo, non-Spanish-speaking teachers are woefully unable to meet. As a result, Spanish-speaking children are often relegated to classes for the mentally retarded, simply because many teachers, wittingly or unwittingly, equate linguistic disadvantage with intellectual deficiency. The percentage of

Mexican American children classified with inferior IQs is two-and-a-half times their ratio to the general population. In California alone, Mexican Americans account for more than 40 percent of the so-called mentally retarded.

Until recently, most educators accepted the results of IQ tests — whether Stanford-Binet, Otis, or SCAT — as accurate measurements of the intellectual capacity of Spanish-speaking Americans, despite the fact that all these tests are given in English and their culture content is biased toward middle-class Anglo America. Only in the last few years have educators become aware that the right instruments are lacking for measuring intelligence and the achievement potential of Mexican Americans, although as long ago as 1935 Herschel T. Manuel had pointed out the deficiencies of the Stanford-Binet. Today most enlightened educators acknowledge the relationship between the amount of retardation and the extent to which intelligence tests require a knowledge of English.

In 1968, as a result of severe criticism from the Association of Mexican American Educators, the California State Board of Education created a special advisory committee to investigate charges that IQ tests seriously hinder some children — especially minority children — in achieving normal educational goals. The findings of the committee are startling. Mexican American children, classified as mentally retarded after IQ tests in English, did remarkably better on tests in Spanish. Some of the children tested had spent as long as three years in special classes for slow learners simply because of low IQ scores. The study by the special advisory committee found that the "special" classes themselves had "a retarding influence." After retesting, one Mexican American student showed an improvement of twenty-eight points, while the group's average rose thirteen points, from seventy to eighty-three. The report of the committee asserts that Mexican American students apparently are placed in remedial or special classes "solely on their ability to function in what is a foreign language."

But the issues cannot be reduced to language alone, for language is only one manifestation of the ethnic bias of the school culture. To imagine such courses as "Speech X" (Corrective Instruction in English Pronunciation) as a palliative or form of remediation for the linguistic ills of Mexican Americans is to treat the symptoms rather than the malady, for the malady is a social one, and not one of grammar or pronunciation.

The teacher, as the central figure in the dynamics of social relations in educational institutions, needs to fully comprehend the nature of language and its psycho-social function in human beings, especially children. He needs to understand, for example, that when Chicano children are punished for breaking "no Spanish" rules, they are being reprimanded for the crime of speaking the only language they know. They are being pressed into thinking of their language as "wrong" and "inferior," and the more this continues the more they become hostile, resentful, and alienated from society, from their families, and even from themselves. Thus, the Spanish-speaking child who encounters stern and imposing prohibitions against using his language not only is traumatized by a conflict he does not readily understand but is forced into a position of repudiating his cultural identity or else of perishing within the educational process.

Only recently have "no Spanish" rules been challenged by Mexican Americans in such cities as San Antonio and El Paso, but only after actual or threatened Mexican American student uprisings. In 1969 the proposed action on the part of the National Education Association to decertify one El Paso high school if it continued its rule of prohibiting Spanish helped resolve the issue there in favor of the Spanish-speaking student population of the city.

Although the "no Spanish" rules are slowly being eliminated, the Anglo-dominated educational systems of the Southwest still tend to culturally emasculate Mexican American youngsters by deliberately squelching Mexican characteristics. José becomes Joe; Jesús becomes Jesse. Mexican American students are told they must accept and assimilate quickly into Anglo culture or face economic and financial deprivation when they are adults. In effect, this is like telling the Mexican American child that there is something wrong in being a Mexican American. And though Spanish may no longer be prohibited on some school grounds, José (Joe) has become more self-conscious of his Spanish and is more and more withdrawn. Not only has he been made to feel marginal in Anglo American society because of his lack of English, but he is made to feel equally marginal in his Spanish-speaking environment.

To eliminate such identity crises, not only must teachers of Mexican Americans become more aware of the Mexican American's heritage and culture, but they must rid themselves of outmoded concepts about language. As Harold Howe, former U.S. Commissioner of Education, put it, "It is time we stopped wasting [our linguistic resources] and instead enabled youngsters to move back and forth from one language to another without any sense of difficulty or strangeness."

RODOLFO GONZALES

I Am Joaquín

In these lines that form the initial section of his epic poem, Rodolfo Gonzales speaks as "Joaquín," summarizing and celebrating the cultural history of the Chicano. Gonzales' forceful lines re-create the social injustice that has been objectively described by such scholars as Philip Ortego and Ernesto Galarza. The founder of the Crusade for Justice in Denver, Colorado, Rodolfo Gonzales is an activist of national prominence in the Chicano movement. His Chicano school and cultural center in Denver attest the spiritual nature of the victory that he seeks.

I am Joaquín,
lost in a world of confusion,
caught up in the whirl of a
                gringo society,
confused by the rules,
scorned by attitudes,
suppressed by manipulation,
and destroyed by modern society.
My fathers
   have lost the economic battle
and won
   the struggle of cultural survival.

And now!
   I must choose
                between
   the paradox of
victory of the spirit,
despite physical hunger,
                or
   to exist in the grasp
of American social neurosis,

sterilization of the soul
and a full stomach.

Yes,
I have come a long way to nowhere,
unwillingly dragged by that
monstrous, technical,
industrial giant called
Progress
and Anglo success. . . .

I look at myself.
I watch my brothers.
I shed tears of sorrow.
I sow seeds of hate.
I withdraw to the safety within the
circle of life —
MY OWN PEOPLE.

LUIS VALDEZ

Los Vendidos

Los Vendidos *("The Sellouts") is one of the early and most popular of the short plays, called "actos," developed and performed by Luis Valdez's Teatro Campesino ("Farmworkers' Theater") in California. The Teatro gave its first performance of* Los Vendidos *in Elysian Park, East Los Angeles, in 1967. The play presents several common stereotypes of the Chicano — stereotypes that exist not only in the minds of many Anglos (non-Chicanos), but in the consciousness of some Chicanos as well. In an unexpected twist at the end, however, the author hints that stereotypical thinking can be turned to the advantage of those who are stereotyped.* Los Vendidos *perfectly exemplifies Valdez's unique blend of comedy and social comment.*

Characters HONEST SANCHO
MISS JIMÉNEZ
FARMWORKER
JOHNNY PACHUCO
REVOLUCIONARIO
MEXICAN AMERICAN

SCENE *Honest Sancho's Used Mexican Lot and Mexican Curio Shop. Three models are on display in Honest Sancho's shop. To the right there is a Revolucionario, complete with sombrero, carrilleras, and carabina*[1] *.30-.30. At center, on the floor, there is the Farmworker, under a broad straw sombrero. At stage left is the Pachuco, filero*[2] *in hand.*

1 *carrilleras; carabina* cartridge belts; rifle
2 *filero* knife (pachuco slang. The pachucos were Chicano youths of the 1940s and 1950s who belonged to street gangs.)

Honest Sancho is moving among his models, dusting them off and preparing for another day of business.

SANCHO Bueno, bueno, mis monos, vamos a ver a quién vendemos ahora, ¿no? *(To audience)* ¡Quihubo! [3] I'm Honest Sancho and this is my shop. I used to be a labor contractor, but now I have my own little business. All I need now is a customer. *(A bell rings offstage.)* Ay, a customer!

SECRETARY *(entering)* Good morning, I'm Miss Jiménez from —

SANCHO Ah, una chicana! Welcome, welcome, Señorita Jiménez.

SECRETARY *(Anglo pronunciation)* *Jim*-enez.

SANCHO ¿Qué? [4]

SECRETARY My name is Miss *Jim*-enez. Don't you speak English? What's wrong with you?

SANCHO Oh, nothing, Señorita *Jim*-enez. I'm here to help you.

SECRETARY That's better. As I was starting to say, I'm a secretary from the state office building, and we're looking for a Mexican type for the administration.

SANCHO Well, you come to the right place, lady. This is Honest Sancho's Used Mexican Lot, and we got all types here. Any particular type you want?

SECRETARY Yes, we were looking for somebody suave —

SANCHO Suave.

SECRETARY Debonair.

SANCHO De buen aire.

SECRETARY Dark.

SANCHO Prieto.

SECRETARY But of course not too dark.

SANCHO No muy prieto.

SECRETARY Perhaps, beige.

SANCHO Beige, just the tone. Así como cafecito con leche, ¿no? [5]

3 *Bueno . . . ¡Quihubo!* Okay, okay, my cute puppets. Let's see which one of you we're going to sell now — right? . . . What's up?
4 *¿Qué?* What?
5 *Así . . . no?* Somewhat like the color of coffee with milk — right?

SECRETARY One more thing. He must be hardworking.

SANCHO That could only be one model. Step right over here to the center of the shop, lady. *(They cross to the Farmworker.)* This is our standard farmworker model. Take special notice of his four-ply Goodyear huaraches, made from the rain tire. This wide-brimmed sombrero is an extra added feature — keeps off the sun, rain, and dust.

SECRETARY Yes, it does look durable.

SANCHO And our farmworker model is friendly. Muy amable.[6] Watch. *(Snaps his fingers.)*

FARMWORKER *(lifts up head)* Buenos días, señorita. *(His head drops.)*

SECRETARY My, he's friendly.

SANCHO Didn't I tell you? Loves his patrones![7] But his most attractive feature is that he's hardworking. Let me show you. *(Snaps fingers. Farmworker stands.)*

FARMWORKER ¡El jale![8] *(He begins to work.)*

SANCHO As you can see, he is cutting grapes.

SECRETARY Oh, I wouldn't know.

SANCHO He also picks cotton. *(Snap. Farmworker begins to pick cotton.)*

SECRETARY Versatile, isn't he?

SANCHO He also picks melons. *(Snap. Farmworker picks melons.)* That's his slow speed for late in the season. Here's his fast speed. *(Snap. Farmworker picks faster.)*

SECRETARY Chihuahua[9] . . . I mean, goodness, he sure is a hard worker.

SANCHO *(pulls the Farmworker to his feet)* And that isn't the half of it. Do you see these little holes on his arms that appear to be pores? During those hot sluggish days in the field when the vines or the branches get so entangled it's almost impossible to move, these

6 *Muy amable.* Very friendly.
7 *patrones* bosses
8 *¡El jale!* Work! (pachuco slang)
9 *Chihuahua* Name of a city and state in the northern part of Mexico, frequently used as a mild expletive much like the English "Holy Toledo"

holes emit a certain grease that allows our model to slip and slide right through the crop with no trouble at all.

SECRETARY Wonderful. But is he economical?

SANCHO Economical? Señorita, you are looking at the Volkswagen of Mexicans. Pennies a day is all it takes. One plate of beans and tortillas will keep him going all day. That, and chile. Plenty of chile. Chile jalapeños, chile verde, chile colorado. But, of course, if you do give him chile *(Snap. Farmworker turns left face. Snap. Farmworker bends over.)*, then you have to change his oil filter once a week.

SECRETARY What about storage?

SANCHO No problem. You know the farm labor camps? They were designed with our model in mind. Five, six, seven, even ten in one of those shacks will give you no trouble at all. You can also put him in old barns, old cars, riverbanks. You can even leave him out in the field overnight with no worry!

SECRETARY Remarkable.

SANCHO And here's an added feature: every year at the end of the season, this model moves on and doesn't return until next spring.

SECRETARY How about that. But tell me, does he speak English?

SANCHO Another outstanding feature is that last year this model was programmed to go out on *strike! (Snap.)*

FARMWORKER ¡HUELGA! ¡HUELGA! Hermanos, sálganse de esos files.[10] *(Snap. He stops.)*

SECRETARY No! Oh no, we can't strike in the state capitol.

SANCHO Well, he also scabs. *(Snap.)*

FARMWORKER Me vendo barato, ¿y qué? [11] *(Snap.)*

SECRETARY That's much better, but you didn't answer my question. Does he speak English?

10 *¡HUELGA! . . . files* STRIKE! STRIKE! Get out of those fields, brothers.

11 *Me . . . qué?* I sell myself cheap — so what?

SANCHO Bueno . . . no, pero[12] he has other —

SECRETARY No.

SANCHO Other features.

SECRETARY *No!* He just won't do!

SANCHO Okay, okay pues.[13] We have other models.

SECRETARY I hope so. What we need is something a little more sophisticated.

SANCHO Sophisti — ¿qué?

SECRETARY An urban model.

SANCHO Ah, from the city! Step right back. Over here in this corner of the shop is exactly what you're looking for. Introducing our new Johnny Pachuco model! This is our fastback model. Streamlined. Built for speed, low-riding, city life. Take a look at some of these features. Mag shoes, dual exhausts, jet black paint-job, dark-tint windshield, a little poof on top. Let me just turn him on. *(Snap. Johnny walks to stage center with a pachuco bounce.)*

SECRETARY What was that?

SANCHO That, señorita, was the Chicano shuffle.

SECRETARY Okay, what does he do?

SANCHO Anything and everything necessary for city life. For instance, survival: he knife-fights. *(Snap. Johnny pulls out switchblade and swings at Secretary.)*

[*Secretary screams.*]

SANCHO He dances. *(Snap.)*

[*Johnny sings and dances. Sancho snaps his fingers.*]

SANCHO And here's a feature no city model can be without. He gets arrested, but not without resisting, of course. *(Snap.)*

JOHNNY I didn't do it! I didn't do it! *(Johnny turns and stands up against an imaginary wall, legs spread out, arms behind his back.)*

SECRETARY Oh no, we can't have arrests! We must maintain law and order.

12 *Bueno . . . pero* Well . . . no, but
13 *pues* then

SANCHO But he's bilingual!

SECRETARY Bilingual?

SANCHO Simón que yes.[14] He speaks English! Johnny, give us some English. *(Snap.)*

JOHNNY *(comes downstage)* Down with whites! Brown power!

SECRETARY *(gasps)* *Oh!* He can't say that!

SANCHO Well, he learned it in your school.

SECRETARY I don't care where he learned it.

SANCHO But he's economical!

SECRETARY Economical?

SANCHO Nickels and dimes. You can keep Johnny running on hamburgers, Taco Bell tacos, Lucky Lager beer, Thunderbird wine, yesca —

SECRETARY ¿Yesca?

SANCHO Mota.

SECRETARY ¿Mota?

SANCHO Leños . . . *Marijuana. (Snap. Johnny inhales on an imaginary joint.)*

SECRETARY That's against the law!

JOHNNY *(big smile, holding his breath)* Yeah.

SANCHO He also snorts coke. *(Snap. Johnny snorts coke. Big smile)*

JOHNNY That's too much, ése.[15]

SECRETARY No, Mr. Sancho, I don't think this —

SANCHO Wait a minute, he has other qualities I know you'll love. For example, an inferiority complex. *(Snap.)*

JOHNNY *(to Sancho)* You think you're better than me, huh, ése? *(Swings switchblade)*

SANCHO He can also be beaten and he bruises; cut him and he bleeds; kick him and he — *(He beats, bruises, and kicks Johnny.)* Would you like to try it?

SECRETARY Oh, I couldn't.

SANCHO Be my guest. He's a great scapegoat.

SECRETARY No really.

SANCHO Please.

14 *Simón que yes.* Yes indeedy. (pachuco slang)
15 *ése* man (pachuco slang)

SECRETARY Well, all right. Just once. *(She kicks Johnny.)* Oh, he's so soft.

SANCHO Wasn't that good? Try again.

SECRETARY *(kicks Johnny)* Oh, he's so wonderful! *(She kicks him again.)*

SANCHO Okay, that's enough, lady. You ruin the merchandise. Yes, our Johnny Pachuco model can give you many hours of pleasure. Why, one police department just bought twenty of these to train their rookie cops on. And talk about maintenance. Señorita, you are looking at an entirely self-supporting machine. You're never going to find our Johnny Pachuco model on the relief rolls. No, sir, this model knows how to liberate.

SECRETARY Liberate?

SANCHO He steals. *(Snap. Johnny rushes the secretary and steals her purse.)*

JOHNNY ¡Dame esa bolsa, vieja![16] *(He grabs the purse and runs. Snap by Sancho. He stops.)*

[*Secretary runs after Johnny and grabs purse away from him, kicking him as she goes.*]

SECRETARY No, no, no! We can't have any *more* thieves in our state administration. Put him back.

SANCHO Okay, we still got other models. Come on, Johnny, we'll sell you to some old lady. *(Sancho takes Johnny back to his place.)*

SECRETARY Mr. Sancho, I don't think you quite understand what we need. What we need is something that will attract the women voters. Something more traditional, more romantic.

SANCHO Ah, a lover. *(He smiles meaningfully.)* Step right over here, señorita. Introducing our standard Revolucionario and/or Early California Bandit type. As you can see, he is well-built, sturdy, durable. This is the International Harvester of Mexicans.

SECRETARY What does he do?

SANCHO You name it, he does it. He rides horses, stays in

16 *¡Dame . . . vieja!* Give me that purse, lady!

the mountains, crosses deserts, plains, rivers, leads revolutions, follows revolutions, kills, can be killed, serves as a martyr, hero, movie star — did I say movie star? Did you ever see *Viva Zapata?*[17] *Viva Villa,*[17] *Villa Rides, Pancho Villa Returns, Pancho Villa Goes Back, Pancho Villa Meets Abbott and Costello* —

SECRETARY I've never seen any of those.

SANCHO Well, he was in all of them. Listen to this. *(Snap.)*

REVOLUCIONARIO *(scream)* ¡VIVA VILLAAAAA!

SECRETARY That's awfully loud.

SANCHO He has a volume control. *(He adjusts volume. Snap.)*

REVOLUCIONARIO *(mousy voice)* viva villa.

SECRETARY That's better.

SANCHO And even if you didn't see him in the movies, perhaps you saw him on TV. He makes commercials. *(Snap.)*

REVOLUCIONARIO Is there a Frito Bandito in your house?

SECRETARY Oh yes, I've seen that one!

SANCHO Another feature about this one is that he is economical. He runs on raw horsemeat and tequila!

SECRETARY Isn't that rather savage?

SANCHO Al contrario,[18] it makes him a lover. *(Snap.)*

REVOLUCIONARIO *(to Secretary)* ¡Ay, mamasota, cochota, ven pa'cá![19] *(He grabs Secretary and folds her back, Latin-lover style.)*

SANCHO *(Snap. Revolucionario goes back upright.)* Now wasn't that nice?

SECRETARY Well, it was rather nice.

SANCHO And finally, there is one outstanding feature about this model I *know* the ladies are going to love: he's a *genuine* antique! He was made in Mexico in 1910!

17 *Zapata; Villa* leaders of revolutionary forces in Mexico in the early 1900s
18 *Al contrario* On the contrary
19 *¡Ay . . . pa'cá!* Oh mama, you cute thing you, come over here!

SECRETARY Made in Mexico?

SANCHO That's right. Once in Tijuana, twice in Guadalajara, three times in Cuernavaca.

SECRETARY Mr. Sancho, I thought he was an American product.

SANCHO No, but —

SECRETARY No, I'm sorry. We can't buy anything but American-made products. He just won't do.

SANCHO But he's an antique!

SECRETARY I don't care. You still don't understand what we need. It's true we need Mexican models such as these, but it's more important that he be *American.*

SANCHO American?

SECRETARY That's right, and judging from what you've shown me, I don't think you have what we want. Well, my lunch hour's almost over, I better —

SANCHO Wait a minute! Mexican but American?

SECRETARY That's correct.

SANCHO Mexican but . . . *(A sudden flash) American!* Yeah, I think we've got exactly what you want. He just came in today! Give me a minute. *(He exits. Talks from backstage)* Here he is in the shop. Let me just get some papers off. There. Introducing our new Mexican American! Ta-ra-ra-ra-ra-RA-RAAA!

[*Sancho brings out the Mexican American model, a clean-shaven middle-class type in a business suit, with glasses.*]

SECRETARY *(impressed)* Where have you been hiding this one?

SANCHO He just came in this morning. Ain't he a beauty? Feast your eyes on him! Sturdy U.S. Steel frame, streamlined, modern. As a matter of fact, he is built exactly like our Anglo models except that he comes in a variety of darker shades: Naugahyde, leather, or leatherette.

SECRETARY Naugahyde.

SANCHO Well, we'll just write that down. Yes, señorita, this model represents the apex of American engineering! He is bilingual, college-educated, ambitious! Say the word *acculturate* and he accelerates. He is intelligent, well-mannered, clean — did I say clean? *(Snap. Mexican American raises his arm.)* Smell.

SECRETARY *(smells)* Old Sobaco,[20] my favorite.

SANCHO *(Snap. Mexican American turns toward Sancho.)* Eric? *(To Secretary)* We call him Eric García. *(To Eric)* I want you to meet Miss *Jim*-enez, Eric.

MEXICAN AMERICAN Miss *Jim*-enez, I am delighted to make your acquaintance. *(He kisses her hand.)*

SECRETARY Oh, my, how charming!

SANCHO Did you feel the suction? He has seven especially engineered suction cups right behind his lips. He's a charmer, all right!

SECRETARY How about boards — does he function on boards?

SANCHO You name them, he is on them. Parole boards, draft boards, school boards, taco quality-control boards, surfboards, two-by-fours.

SECRETARY Does he function in politics?

SANCHO Señorita, you are looking at a political *machine.* Have you ever heard of the OEO, EEOC, COD, War on Poverty? That's our model! Not only that, he makes political speeches.

SECRETARY May I hear one?

SANCHO With pleasure. *(Snap.)* Eric, give us a speech.

MEXICAN AMERICAN Mr. Congressman, Mr. Chairman, members of the board, honored guests, ladies and gentlemen. *(Sancho and Secretary applaud.)* Please, please. I come before you as a Mexican American to tell you about the problems of the Mexican. The problems of the Mexican stem from one thing and one thing alone: he's stupid. He's uneducated. He needs to stay in school. He needs to be ambitious, forward-looking, harder-working. He needs to think American, American, American, AMERICAN, AMERICAN, AMERICAN. GOD BLESS AMERICA! GOD BLESS AMERICA! GOD BLESS AMERICA!! *(He goes out of control.)*

20 *Old Sobaco* Old Armpit

[*Sancho snaps frantically and the Mexican American finally slumps forward, bending at the waist.*]

SECRETARY Oh my, he's patriotic too!

SANCHO Sí, señorita, he loves his country. Let me just make a little adjustment here. *(Stands Mexican American up)*

SECRETARY What about upkeep? Is he economical?

SANCHO Well, no, I won't lie to you. The Mexican American costs a little bit more, but you get what you pay for. He's worth every extra cent. You can keep him running on dry Martinis and steaks.

SECRETARY Apple pie?

SANCHO Only Mom's. Of course, he's also programmed to eat Mexican food at ceremonial functions, but I must warn you: an overdose of beans will plug up his exhaust.

SECRETARY Fine! There's just one more question: *How much do you want for him?*

SANCHO Well, I tell you what I'm gonna do. Today and today only, because you've been so sweet, I'm gonna let you steal this model from me! I'm gonna let you drive him off the lot for the simple price of — let's see, taxes and license included — fifteen thousand dollars.

SECRETARY Fifteen thousand *dollars?* For a *Mexican?*

SANCHO Mexican? What are you talking, lady? This is a Mexican *American!* We had to melt down two pachucos, a farmworker, and three gabachos[21] to make this model! You want quality, but you gotta pay for it! This is no cheap runabout. He's got class!

SECRETARY Okay, I'll take him.

SANCHO You will?

SECRETARY Here's your money.

SANCHO You mind if I count it?

SECRETARY Go right ahead.

SANCHO Well, you'll get your pink slip in the mail. Oh, do you want me to wrap him up for you? We have a box in the back.

21 *gabachos* Anglos

SECRETARY No, thank you. There's going to be a luncheon this afternoon, and we need a brown face in the crowd. How do I drive him?

SANCHO Just snap your fingers. He'll do anything you want.

[*Secretary snaps. Mexican American steps forward.*]

MEXICAN AMERICAN ¡RAZA QUERIDA, VAMOS LEVANTANDO ARMAS PARA LIBERARNOS DE ESTOS DESGRACIADOS GABACHOS QUE NOS EXPLOTAN! VAMOS —[22]

SECRETARY What did he say?

SANCHO Something about lifting arms, killing white people, and so on.

SECRETARY But he's not supposed to say that!

SANCHO Look, lady, don't blame me for bugs from the factory. He's your Mexican American, you bought him, now drive him off the lot!

SECRETARY But he's broken!

SANCHO Try snapping another finger.

[*Secretary snaps. Mexican American comes to life again.*]

MEXICAN AMERICAN ¡ESTA GRAN HUMANIDAD HA DICHO BASTA! ¡Y SE HA PUESTO EN MARCHA! ¡BASTA! ¡BASTA! ¡VIVA LA RAZA! ¡VIVA LA CAUSA! ¡VIVA LA HUELGA! ¡VIVAN LOS BROWN BERETS! ¡VIVAN LOS ESTUDIANTES![23] CHICANO POWER!

[*The Mexican American turns toward the Secretary, who gasps and backs up. He keeps turning toward*

22 *¡RAZA . . . VAMOS —* Beloved Chicano people, let us take up arms to liberate ourselves from these despicable Anglos that exploit us! Let us —

23 *¡ESTA . . . ESTUDIANTES!* This great mass of humanity has said, Enough! And it has begun to march forth! Enough! Enough! Long live the Chicano people! Long live La Causa! Long live the strike! Long live the Brown Berets! Long live the students!

the Pachuco, Farmworker, and Revolucionario, snapping his fingers and turning each of them on, one by one.]

JOHNNY *(Snap. To Secretary)* I'm going to get you, baby! Viva la Raza!

FARMWORKER *(Snap. To Secretary)* ¡Viva la huelga! *¡Viva la huelga!* ¡VIVA LA HUELGA!

REVOLUCIONARIO *(Snap. To Secretary)* ¡Viva la revolución! ¡VIVA LA REVOLUCION!

[*The three models join together and advance toward the Secretary, who backs up and runs out of the shop screaming. Sancho is at the other end of the shop holding his money in his hand. All freeze. After a few seconds of silence, the Pachuco moves and stretches, shaking his arms and loosening up. The Farmworker and Revolucionario do the same. Sancho stays where he is, frozen to his spot.*]

JOHNNY Man, that was a long one, ése. *(Others agree with him.)*

FARMWORKER How did we do?

JOHNNY Perty good, look all that lana,[24] man! *(He goes over to Sancho and removes the money from his hand. Sancho stays where he is.)*

REVOLUCIONARIO Look at all the money.

JOHNNY We keep this up, we're going to be rich.

FARMWORKER They think we're machines.

REVOLUCIONARIO Burros.

JOHNNY Puppets.

MEXICAN AMERICAN The only thing I don't like is, how come I always got to play the Mexican American?

JOHNNY That's what you get for finishing high school.

FARMWORKER How about our wages, ése?

JOHNNY Here it comes right now. Three thousand dollars for you, three thousand for you, three thousand for you, and three thousand for me. The rest we put back into the business.

24 *lana* money (colloquial; literally, "wool")

MEXICAN AMERICAN Too much, man. Hey, where you vatos[25] going tonight?

FARMWORKER I'm going over to Concha's. There's a party.

JOHNNY Wait a minute, vatos. What about our salesman? I think he needs an oil job.

REVOLUCIONARIO Leave him to me.

[*The Pachuco, Farmworker, and Mexican American exit, talking loudly about their plans for the night. The Revolucionario goes over to Sancho, removes his derby hat and cigar, lifts him up and throws him over his shoulder. Sancho hangs loose, lifeless.*]

REVOLUCIONARIO *(to audience)* He's the best model we got! *(Exit.)*

25 *vatos* guys; dudes (pachuco slang)

El Barrio

The Barrio

in the barrios
of my homeland . . .
all those cities
like el paso, los angeles,
albuquerque,
denver, san antonio

Ricardo Sánchez

RASPAS con NIEVE
BARBACOA
TODOS LOS
DOMINGOS
CARMEN LOMAS GARZA

Ernesto Galarza

On the Edge of the Barrio

In this excerpt from his autobiography, Barrio Boy, *a distinguished scholar recalls people and events from his adolescence. Ernesto Galarza had come to the Sacramento barrio with his mother and uncles from a mountain village in the Mexican state of Nayarit, where he was born in 1905. From the schools and jobs that he describes in "The Edge of the Barrio," he went on to Occidental College, Stanford, and Columbia. In time Galarza became a labor organizer and union consultant as well as a teacher, sociologist, and writer — and the outstanding authority on Mexican emigrants, farm labor history, and what has come to be known as "agribusiness." Dr. Galarza's* Merchants of Labor *and* Spiders in the House and Workers in the Field *are regarded as classic studies.*

I had been reading stories in the *Sacramento Bee* of the Spanish influenza. At first it was far off, like the war, in places such as New York and Texas. Then the stories told of people dying in California towns we knew, and finally the *Bee* began reporting the spread of the flu in our city.

One Sunday morning we saw Uncle Gustavo coming down the street with a suitcase in his hand, walking slowly. I ran out to meet him. By the front gate he dropped the suitcase, leaned on the fence, and fainted. He had been working as a sandhog on the American River, and had come home weak from fever.

Gustavo was put to bed in one of the front rooms. Uncle José set out to look for a doctor, who came the next day, weary and nearly sick himself. He ordered Gustavo to the hospital. Three days later I answered the telephone call from the hospital telling us he was dead. Only José went to Gustavo's funeral. The rest of us, except my stepfather, were sick in bed with the fever.

In the dining room, near the windows where the sunlight would warm her, my mother lay on a cot, a kerosene stove at her feet. The day Gustavo died she was delirious. José bicycled all over the city, looking for oranges, which the doctor said were the best medicine we could give her. I sweated out the fever, nursed by José, who brought me glasses of steaming lemonade and told me my mother was getting better. The children were quarantined in another room, lightly touched by the fever, more restless than sick.

Late one afternoon José came into my room, wrapped me in blankets, pulled a cap over my ears, and carried me to my mother's bedside. My stepfather was holding a hand mirror to her lips. It didn't fog. She had stopped breathing. In the next room my sister was singing to the other children, "A birdie with a yellow bill/hopped upon my windowsill,/cocked a shiny eye, and said,/'Shame on you, you sleepyhead.' "

The day we buried my mother, Mrs. Dodson took the oldest sister home with her. The younger children were sent to a neighbor. That night José went to the barrio, got drunk, borrowed a pistol, and was arrested for shooting up Second Street.

A month later I made a bundle of the family keepsakes my stepfather allowed me to have, including the butterfly sarape, my books, and some family pictures. With the bundle tied to the bars of my bicycle, I pedaled to the basement room José had rented for the two of us on O Street near the corner of Fifth, on the edge of the barrio.

José was now working the riverboats and, in the slack season, following the round of odd jobs about the city. In our basement room, with a kitchen closet, bathroom, and laundry tub on the back porch and a woodshed for storage, I kept house. We bought two cots, one for me and the other for José when he was home.

Our landlords lived upstairs, a middle-aged brother and sister who worked and rented rooms. They were friends of doña Tránsito, the grandmother of a Mexican family that lived in a weather-beaten cottage on the corner. Doña Tránsito was in her sixties, round as a barrel, and she wore her gray hair in braids and smoked hand-rolled cigarettes on her rickety front porch. Living only three houses from doña Tránsito, saying my saludos to her every time I passed the corner, I lived inside a circle of security when José was away.

José had chosen our new home because it was close to the Hearkness Junior High School, to which I transferred from Bret Harte. As the jefe de familia[1] he explained that I could help earn our living but that I was to study for a high school diploma. That being settled, my routine was clearly divided into school time and work time, the second depending on when I was free from the first.

Few Mexicans of my age from the barrio were enrolled at the junior high school when I went there. At least, there were no other Mexican boys or girls in Mr. Everett's class in civics, or Miss Crowley's English composition, or Mrs. Stevenson's Spanish course. Mrs. Stevenson assigned me to read to the class and to recite poems by Amado Nervo, because the poet was from Tepic and I was, too. Miss Crowley accepted my compositions about Jalcocotán and the buried treasure of Acaponeta while the others in the class were writing about Sir Patrick Spence and the Beautiful Lady Without Mercy, whom they had never met. For Mr. Everett's class, the last of the day, I clipped pieces from the *Sacramento Bee* about important events in Sacramento. From him I learned to use the ring binder in which I kept clippings to prepare oral reports. Occasionally he kept me after school to talk. He sat on his desk, one leg dangling over a corner, behind him the frame of a large window and the arching elms of the school yard, telling me he thought I could easily make the debating team at the high school next year, that Stanford University might be the place to go after graduation, and making other by-the-way comments that began to shape themselves into my future.

1 *jefe de familia* head of the household (literally, "head of the family")

Afternoons, Saturdays, and summers allowed me many hours of work time I did not need for study. José explained how things now stood. There were two funerals to pay for. He would pay the rent and buy the food. My clothes, books, and school expenses would be up to me.

On my vacations and when he was not on the riverboats, he found me a job as water boy on a track gang. We chopped wood together near Woodland and stacked empty lug boxes in a cannery yard. Cleaning vacant houses and chopping weeds were jobs we could do as a team when better ones were not to be had. As the apprentice, I learned from him how to brace myself for a heavy lift, to lock my knee under a loaded hand-truck, to dance rather than lift a ladder, and to find the weakest grain in a log. Like him I spit into my palms to get the feel of the ax handle and grunted as the blade bit into the wood. Imitating him, I circled a tree several times, sizing it up, tanteando, as he said, before pruning or felling it.

Part of one summer my uncle worked on the river while I hired out as a farmhand on a small ranch south of Sacramento. My senior on the place was Roy, a husky Oklahoman who was a part-time taxi driver and a full-time drinker of hard whiskey. He was heavy-chested, heavy-lipped, and jowly, a grumbler rather than a talker and a man of great ingenuity with tools and automobile engines. Under him I learned to drive the Fordson tractor on the place, man the gasoline pump, feed the calves, check an irrigation ditch, make lug boxes for grapes, and many other tasks on a small farm.

Roy and I sat under the willow tree in front of the ranch house after work, I on the grass, he on a creaky wicker chair, a hulking, sour man glad for the company of a boy. He counseled me on how to avoid the indulgences he was so fond of, beginning his sentences with a phrase he repeated over and over, "as the feller says." "Don't aim to tell you your business," he explained, "but as the feller says, get yourself a good woman, don't be no farmhand for a livin', be a lawyer or a doctor, and don't get to drinkin' nohow. And there's another thing, Ernie. If nobody won't listen to you, go on and talk to yourself and hear what a smart man has to say."

And Roy knew how to handle boys, which he showed in an episode that could have cost me my life or my self-confidence. He had taught me to drive the tractor, walking alongside during the lessons as I maneuvered it, shifting gears, stopping and starting, turning and backing, raising a cloud of dust wherever we went. Between drives Roy told me about the different working parts of the machine, giving me instructions on oiling and greasing and filling the radiator. "She needs to be took care of, Ernie," he admonished me, "like a horse. And another thing, she's like to buck. She can turn clear over on you if you let 'er. If she starts to lift from the front even a mite, you turn her off. You hear?"

"Yes, sir," I said, meaning to keep his confidence in me as a good tractor man.

It was a few days after my first solo drive that it happened. I was rounding a telephone pole on the slightly sloping bank of the irrigation ditch. I swung around too fast for one of the rear tracks to keep its footing. It spun and the front began to lift. Forgetting Roy's emphatic instructions, I gunned the engine, trying to right us to the level ground above the ditch. The tractor's nose kept climbing in front of me. We slipped against the pole, the tractor bucking, as Roy said it would.

Roy's warning broke through to me in my panic, and I reached up to turn off the ignition. My bronco's engine sputtered out and it settled on the ground with a thump.

I sat for a moment in my sweat. Roy was coming down the ditch in a hurry. He walked up to me and with a quick look saw that neither I nor the tractor was damaged.

"Git off," he said.

I did, feeling that I was about to be demoted, stripped of my rank, bawled out, and fired.

Roy mounted the machine, started it, and worked it off the slope to flat ground. Leaving the engine running, he said: "Git on."

I did.

"Now finish the disking," he said. Above the clatter of the machine he said: "Like I said, she can buck. If she does, cut 'er. You hear?" And he waved me off to my work.

Except for food and a place to live, with which José provided me, I was on my own. Between farm jobs I worked in town, adding to my experience as well as to my income. As a clerk in a drugstore on Second and J, in the heart of the lower part of town, I waited on Chicanos who spoke no English and who came in search of remedies with no prescription other than a recital of their pains. I dispensed capsules, pills, liniments, and emulsions as instructed by the pharmacist, who glanced at our customers from the back of the shop and diagnosed their ills as I translated them. When I went on my shift, I placed a card in the window that said "Se habla español." So far as my Chicano patients were concerned, it might as well have said "Dr. Ernesto Galarza."

From drugs I moved to office supplies and stationery sundries, working as delivery boy for Wahl's, several blocks uptown from skid row. Between deliveries I had no time to idle. I helped the stock clerk, took inventory, polished desks, and hopped when a clerk bawled an order down the basement steps. Mr. Wahl, our boss, a stocky man with a slight paunch, strutted a little as he constantly checked on the smallest details of his establishment, including myself. He was always pleasant and courteous, a man in whose footsteps I might possibly walk into the business world of Sacramento.

But like my uncles, I was looking for a better chanza, which I thought I found with Western Union, as a messenger, where I could earn tips as well as wages. Since I knew the lower part of town thoroughly, whenever the telegrams were addressed to that quarter the dispatcher gave them to me. Deliveries to the suites on the second floor of saloons paid especially well, with tips of a quarter from the ladies who worked there. My most generous customer was tall and beautiful Miss Irene, who always asked how I was doing in school. It was she who gave me an English dictionary, the first I ever possessed, a black bound volume with remarkable little scallops on the pages that made it easy to find words. Half smiling, half commanding, Miss Irene said to me more than once: "Don't you stop school without letting me know." I meant to take her advice as earnestly as I took her twenty-five-cent tip.

It was in the lower town also that I nearly became a performing artist. My instructor on the violin had stopped giving me lessons after we moved to Oak Park. When we were back on O Street he sent word through José that I could work as second fiddler on Saturday nights in the dance hall where he played with a mariachi. Besides, I could resume my lessons with him. A dollar a night for two hours as a substitute was the best wages I had ever made. Coached by my teacher, I second-fiddled for sporting Chicanos who swung their ladies on the dance floor and sang to our music. Unfortunately I mentioned my new calling to Miss Crowley when I proposed it to her as a subject for a composition. She kept me after school and persuaded me to give it up, on the ground that I could earn more decorating Christmas cards during the vacation than at the dance hall. She gave me the first order for fifty cards and got subscriptions for me from the other teachers. I spent my Christmas vacation as an illustrator, with enough money saved to quit playing in the saloon.

It was during the summer vacation that school did not interfere with making a living — the time of the year when I went with other barrio people to the ranches to look for work. Still too young to shape up with the day-haul gangs, I loitered on skid row, picking up conversation and reading the chalk signs about work that was being offered. For a few days of picking fruit or pulling hops I bicycled to Folsom, Lodi, Woodland, Freeport, Walnut Grove, Marysville, Slough House, Florin, and places that had no name. Looking for work, I pedaled through a countryside blocked off, mile after mile, into orchards, vineyards, and vegetable farms. Along the ditch banks, where the grass, the morning glory, and the wild oats made a soft mattress, I unrolled my bindle and slept.

In the labor camps I shared the summertime of the

lives of the barrio people. They gathered from barrios of faraway places like Imperial Valley, Los Angeles, Phoenix, and San Antonio. Each family traveling on its own, they came in trucks piled with household goods or packed in their secondhand fotingos[2] and chevees. The trucks and cars were ancient models, fresh out of a used-car lot, with license tags of many states. It was into these jalopies that much of the care and a good part of the family's earnings went. In camp they were constantly being fixed, so close to scrap that when we needed a part for repairs, we first went to the nearest junkyard.

It was a world different in so many ways from the lower part of Sacramento and the residences surrounded by trim lawns and cool canopies of elms to which I had delivered packages for Wahl's. Our main street was usually an irrigation ditch, the water supply for cooking, drinking, laundering, and bathing. In the better camps there was a faucet or a hydrant, from which water was carried in buckets, pails, and washtubs. If the camp belonged to a contractor and it was used from year to year, there were permanent buildings — a shack for his office, the privies, weatherworn and sagging, and a few cabins made of secondhand lumber, patched and unpainted.

If the farmer provided housing himself, it was in tents pitched on the bare baked earth or on the rough ground of newly plowed land on the edge of a field. Those who arrived late for the work season camped under trees or raised lean-tos along a creek, roofing their trucks with canvas to make bedrooms. Such camps were always well away from the house of the ranchero, screened from the main road by an orchard or a grove of eucalyptus. I helped to pitch and take down such camps, on some spot that seemed lonely when we arrived, desolate when we left.

If they could help it, the workers with families avoided the more permanent camps, where the seasonal hired hands from skid row were more likely to be found. I lived a few days in such a camp and found out why families avoided

2 *fotingos* old cars (often travel-worn Fords)

them. On Saturday nights when the crews had a week's wages in their pockets, strangers appeared, men and women, carrying suitcases with liquor and other contraband. The police were called by the contractor only when the carousing threatened to break into fighting. Otherwise, the weekly bouts were a part of the regular business of the camp.

Like all the others, I often went to work without knowing how much I was going to be paid. I was never hired by a rancher, but by a contractor or a straw boss who picked up crews in town and handled the payroll. The important questions that were in my mind — the wages per hour or per lug box, whether the beds would have mattresses and blankets, the price of meals, how often we would be paid — were never discussed, much less answered, beforehand. Once we were in camp, owing the employer for the ride to the job, having no means to get back to town except by walking and no money for the next meal, arguments over working conditions were settled in favor of the boss. I learned firsthand the chiseling techniques of the contractors and their pushers — how they knocked off two or three lugs of grapes from the daily record for each member of the crew, or the way they had of turning the face of the scales away from you when you weighed your work in.

There was never any doubt about the contractor and his power over us. He could fire a man and his family on the spot and make them wait days for their wages. A man could be forced to quit by assigning him regularly to the thinnest pickings in the field. The worst thing one could do was to ask for fresh water on the job, regardless of the heat of the day; instead of iced water, given freely, the crews were expected to buy sodas at twice the price in town, sold by the contractor himself. He usually had a pistol — to protect the payroll, so it was said. Through the ranchers for whom he worked, we were certain that he had connections with the Autoridades, for they never showed up in camp to settle wage disputes or listen to our complaints or to go for a doctor when one was needed. Lord of a ragtag labor camp of Mexicans, the contractor, a Mexican himself, knew that few men would let their anger blow, even when he stung them with curses.

As a single worker, I usually ate with some household, paying for my board. I did more work than a child but less than a man — neither the head nor the tail of a family. Unless the camp was a large one, I became acquainted with most of the families. Those who could not write asked me to chalk their payroll numbers on the boxes they picked. I counted matches for a man who transferred them from the right pocket of his pants to the left as he tallied the lugs he filled throughout the day. It was his only check on the record the contractor kept of his work. As we worked the rows or the tree blocks during the day, or talked in the evenings where the men gathered in small groups to smoke and rest, I heard about barrios I had never seen but that must have been much like ours in Sacramento.

The only way to complain or protest was to leave, but now and then a camp would stand instead of run, and for a few hours or a few days work would slow down or stop. I saw it happen in a pear orchard in Yolo when pay rates were cut without notice to the crew. The contractor said the market for pears had dropped and the rancher could not afford to pay more. The fruit stayed on the trees while we, a committee drafted by the camp, argued with the contractor first and then with the rancher. The talks gave them time to round up other pickers. A carload of police in plain clothes drove into the camp. We were lined up for our pay, taking whatever the contractor said was on his books. That afternoon we were ordered off the ranch.

In a camp near Folsom, during hop picking, it was not wages but death that pulled the people together. Several children in the camp were sick with diarrhea; one had been taken to the hospital in town and the word came back that he had died. It was the women who guessed that the cause of the epidemic was the water. For cooking and drinking and washing it came from a ditch that went by the ranch stables upstream.

I was appointed by a camp committee to go to Sacramento to find some Autoridad who would send an inspector. Pedaling my bicycle, mulling over where to go and what to say, I remembered some clippings from the *Sacramento Bee* that Mr. Everett had discussed in class, and I decided the man to look for was Mr. Simon Lubin, who was in some way a state Autoridad.

He received me in his office at Weinstock and Lubin's. He sat, square-shouldered and natty, behind a desk with a glass top. He was half-bald, with a strong nose and a dimple in the center of his chin. To his right was a box with small levers into which Mr. Lubin talked and out of which came voices.

He heard me out, asked me questions, and made notes on a pad. He promised that an inspector would come to the camp. I thanked him and thought the business of my visit was over; but Mr. Lubin did not break the handshake until he had said to tell the people in the camp to organize. "Only by organizing," he told me, "will they ever have decent places to live."

I reported the interview with Mr. Lubin to the camp. The part about the inspector they understood and it was voted not to go back to work until he came. The part about organizing was received in silence, and I made my first organizing speech.

The inspector came and a water tank pulled by mules was parked by the irrigation ditch. At the same time the contractor began to fire some of the pickers. I was one of them. I finished that summer nailing boxes on a grape ranch near Florin.

When my job ended, I pedaled back to Sacramento, detouring over country lanes I knew well. Here and there I walked the bicycle over dirt roads rutted by wagons. The pastures were sunburned and the grain fields had been cut to stubble. Riding by a thicket of reeds where an irrigation ditch swamped, I stopped and looked at the red-winged blackbirds riding gracefully on the tips of the canes. Now and then they streaked out of the green clump, spraying the pale sky with crimson dots in all directions.

Crossing the Y Street levee by Southside Park, I rode

through the barrio to doña Tránsito's, leaving my bike hooked on the picket fence by the handlebar.

I knocked on the screen door that always hung tired, like the sagging porch coming unnailed. No one was at home.

It was two hours before time to cook supper. From the stoop I looked up and down the cross streets. The barrio seemed empty.

I unhooked the bicycle, mounted it, and headed for the main high school, twenty blocks away, where I would be going in a week. Pumping slowly, I wondered about the debating team and the other things Mr. Everett had mentioned.

JOHN RECHY

El Paso del Norte

The gateway area known for 375 years as El Paso del Norte ("The Pass of the North") is today the twin cities of El Paso, Texas, and Ciudad Juárez, Mexico. The Rio Grande forms the boundary between them. In these excerpts from a longer essay first published in 1958, John Rechy writes about the distinctive culture of the El Paso barrio, including that of the pachucos — Chicano youths of the 1940s and 1950s who belonged to street gangs. At the same time Rechy gives an occasional glimpse of the border landscape and of what he calls Big Texas. The author was raised in the barrio he describes but has lived all over the United States. He has published both fiction and nonfiction extensively.

This is about El Paso (and Juárez: the Southwest), which so long was just a hometown to me and which now is different from any other section in America.

El Paso and Juárez are in the middle of the Texas, New Mexico, and Mexico white, white desert surrounded by that range of mountains jutting unevenly along the border. At sundown the fat sun squats on the horizon like a Mexican lady grandly on her frontporch. Appropriately.

Because only geographically the Rio Grande, which in the Southwest is a river only part of the time and usually just a strait of sand along the banks of which sick spiders weave their webs, divides the United States from Mexico. Only geographically. The Mexican people of El Paso, more than half the population — and practically all of Smeltertown, Canutillo, Ysleta — are all and always and completely Mexican, and will be. They speak only Spanish to each other and when they say the Capital they mean Mexico DF.[1]

1 *Mexico DF* Mexico City is located in the Distrito Federal.

The Mexicans live concentrated on the Southside of El Paso largely, crowded into tenements, with the walls outside plastered with old Vote-for signs from years back and advertisements of Mexican movies at the Colón — the torn clothes just laundered waving on rickety balconies along Paisano Drive held up God knows how. Or if not, in the Government projects, which are clean tenements — a section for the Mexicans, a section for the Negroes. Politely. Row after row of identical box-houses speckled with dozens and dozens of children.

So this, the Southside, is of course the area of the Mean gangs. The ones on the other side are not as dangerous, of course, because they are mostly Blond and mostly normal Anglo American kiddies growing up naturally and what can you expect? Like the ones from Kern Place — all pretty clean houses at the foot of Mount Franklin — and if those kiddies carry switchblade knives, at least they keep them clean, and when they wear boots, they are Cowboy Boots.

The Southside gangs — that's a different thing. Theyre black-haired. And tense. Mean and bad, with Conflict seething. El Paso's Southside (the Second Ward) gave birth to the internationally famous Pachucos. (Paso — Pacho.) They used to call them boogies, marijuanos, the zoot suits — and the baggy pants with the pegged ankles were boogiepants, and, man, those tigers walked cool, long graceful bad strides, rhythmic as hell, hands deep into pockets, shoulders hunched. Much heart. They really did wear and still sometimes do those hats that Al Capp draws — and the chains, too, from the belt to the pocket in a long loop.

And sitting talking Mexican jive, mano,[2] under the El Paso streetlamps along Hill and Magoffin and Seventh, around Bowie High School and next to the Palace Theater digging Presley and Chuck Berry and Fats Domino, outside the dingy forty-watt-bulb-lighted Southside grocery stores, avoiding la jura,[3] the neo-Pachucos with dreamy junk eyes and their chicks in tight skirts and giant pom-

2 *mano* brother (short for hermano)
3 *la jura* police (pachuco slang)

padours and revealing 1940-style sweaters hang in the steamy El Paso nights, hunched, mean and bad, plotting protest, unconscious of, though they carry it, the burden of the world, and additionally, the burden of Big Texas.

Well, look. In East Texas. In Balmorhea, say. In Balmorhea, with its giant outdoor swimming pool (where that summer the two blond tigers and I went swimming, climbed over the wall and into the rancid-looking night water), there were signs in the two-bit restaurant, in Balmorhea-town then, that said WE DO NOT SERVE MEXICANS, NIGGERS, OR DOGS. That night we went to the hick movie, and the man taking the tickets said, You boys be sure and sit on the right side, the left is for spics. So I said I was on the wrong side and walked out. Later at Kit's aunt's ranch, the aunt waited until the Mexican servant walked out and then said, miserably, Ah jaist caint even eat when they are around. And because earlier had made me feel suddenly a Crusader and it was easy now, I walked out of the dining-room and said well then I shouldnt be here to louse up your dinner, lady.

And you never know it — to look at that magnificent Texas sky.

At Christmas is when Mexican El Paso is magnificent. I dont mean the jazz at San Jacinto Plaza (trees and lights and Christmas carols and Santa Claus). I mean the Southside Christmas. A lot of them — most of them, in fact — put up trees, of course, but many of them put up nacimientos. My father used to start putting ours up almost a month before Christmas when we lived on Wyoming Street. It's a large boxlike thing — ours was, anyway — about six feet wide, six feet tall, eight feet deep, like a room minus the front wall (the minus faces the windows, which are cleaned to sparkle), and inside is a Christmas scene. Ours had the manger and the Virgin of course and St Joseph, and angels hanging from strings floating on angelhair clouds. To the sides of the manger were modern-looking California miniature houses, with real lights in them — some had swimming pools. And stone mountains. On one was the Devil, red, with a wired neck so that the slightest movement made it twitch, drinking out of a bottle. Christ was coming, and naturally the Devil would be feeling low. My father painted an elaborate Texas-like sky behind the manger, with clouds, giant moon, the works — lights all over, and he enclosed the boxlike nacimiento with Christmas-tree branches, and then, one year, he had a real lake — that is, real water which we changed daily. The wise men on their way. Christmas lights, bulbs, on top. He moved the wise men each night, closer to the manger. The Christchild wasnt there yet — He wasnt born. Then on Christmas Eve everyone came over. My mother led the rosary. We all knelt. Someone had been chosen to be the padrino — the godfather — of the Christchild to be born that night. He carried the Child in his hands, everyone kissed it ("adored" it), and then finally He was put into the manger, in the hay. We prayed some more. "Dios te salve, María, llena eres de gracia. . . ."[4] At the stroke of midnight, the Child was born. Then there was a party — tamales, buñuelos,[5] liquor.

At dawn, on a lady's birthday — even now and in El Paso — five or six men gather outside her window, singing and playing their guitars. The sun is about to come out. They sing softly,

Estas son las mañanitas
Que cantaba el Rey David.
A las muchachas bonitas
Se las cantaba él así. . . .[6]

Now the lady comes coyly to the window, standing there until they have finished the soft dawn singing. Now all the neighbors' windows are up and everyone is listening. (No one thinks of calling the police.) Then the lady invites the serenaders inside, and they all have early-morning

4 *"Dios . . . gracia. . . ."* "Hail, Mary, full of grace. . . ."
5 *buñuelos* sweet fritters
6 *Estas . . . así. . . .* This is the tune sung in dawning morning,/The tune King David would sing/To the fairest of maidens./He would sing to them like this. . . .

coffee, pan de dulce, menudo.[7] Then the sun is up in the sky.

The Southwest sky. Beautiful and horrifying. And therefore Wonderful.

Because in all the blunder and bluster of Texas about the wrong things, one thing is really so. The sky.

When it is beautiful it is depthless blue. The sky in other places is like an inverted cup, this shade of blue or gray or black or another shade, with limits, like a painted room. Not in the Southwest. The sky is really millions and millions of miles deep of blue — and in summer, clear magic electric blue.

(How many stars are there in the sky? was our favorite six-year-old children riddle. The answer: cincuenta. Which means fifty, but also: countless. And it's true, so true.)

Before the summer storms, the clouds mass and roll twisting in the sky clashing fiercely, sweeping grandly across the sky. Then giant mushrooms explode. The sky groans, opens, it pours rain.

But before the windstorms, everything is calm, and then a strange ominous mass of gray gathers in the horizon. Then swiftly, in a moment it seems, blowing with the wind, the steel clouds cover the sky, and youre locked down here, so lonesome suddenly youre cold. The wind comes. The tumbleweeds rush with it.

And always there's the fearful wailing.

7 *pan de dulce; menudo* sweet bread; a dish made of tripe

TINO VILLANUEVA

Pachuco Remembered

Unknown to some and nearly forgotten by others, the pachuco of the forties and fifties has nonetheless endured in the memory of many Chicanos, assuming a special place in the imagination of such contemporary writers as José Montoya and Tino Villanueva. In this poem the pachuco's life-style — which included a flamboyant type of dress, a distinctive slang, and a fierce loyalty to his gang — is viewed as an early expression of unrecognized social protest. "Pachuco Remembered" appears in the "Mi Raza" section of Villanueva's 1972 poetry collection.

¡Ese! [1]
Within your will-to-be culture,
incisive,
aguzado,[2]
clutching the accurate click &
fist-warm slash of your filero[3]
(hardened equalizer gave you life,
opened up countercultures U.S.A.).

Precursor.

Vato loco alivianado[4] — a legend in your
own time flaunting early mod, sleazy,
but rigid,
with a message,
in a movement of your own,

1 *¡Ese!* Hey, man! (pachuco slang) 2 *aguzado* shrewd, cunning (pachuco slang) 3 *filero* knife (pachuco slang) 4 *Vato loco alivianado* Crazy, hep dude (pachuco slang)

in your gait sauntering,
swaying,
leaning the wrong way
in assertion.

Baroque carriage between
waving-to-the-wind ducktails &
double-sole calcos[5]
buttressing street corners as any would-be
pillar of society.
Aesthetics existential:
la lisa[6] unbuttoned,
zoot suit with pegged tramos,[7]
a thin belt holding up the
scars of your age —
a moving target for la jura[8] brutality;
brown anathema of high-school principals.
Your fierce stance
vs.
starched voices:

"Take those taps off!"
"Speak English damn it!"
"Button up your shirt!"
"When did you last cut your hair?"
"Coach, give this punk 25 licks!"

Emotion surging silent on your stoic tongue;
machismo-ego punished, feeling your fearful
eyes turn blue in their distant stare.

5 *calcos* shoes (pachuco slang) 6 *la lisa* shirt (pachuco slang)
7 *tramos* trousers (pachuco slang) 8 *la jura* the police (pachuco slang)

Day to day into the night, back to back grief,
& the railroad tracks a /Meskin/Dixon line/
hyphenating
the skin of your accent.
Sirol,[9] you heard the train on time
                                        tearing
through every map of hope SW U.S.A.,
but your poised blood, aware, in a
bitter coming-of-age: a juvenile La Causa
in your wicked
                    stride . . .

9 *Sirol* Yes (pachuco slang)

DANNY SANTIAGO

The Somebody

From a California author comes this short story of the Eastside barrio of Los Angeles. The story is deceptive: seemingly lighthearted, it appears to describe a typical day in the life of Chato, its narrator. But before long the reader becomes aware that Chato is not a typical barrio youth and that he is describing a very significant day in his life — a day when he made a decision that was to have many implications.

This is Chato talking, Chato de Shamrock, from the Eastside in old L.A., and I want you to know this is a big day in my life because today I quit school and went to work as a writer. I write on fences or buildings or anything that comes along. I write my name, not the one I got from my father. I want no part of him. I write Chato, which means Catface, because I have a flat nose like a cat. It's a Mexican word because that's what I am, a Mexican, and I'm not ashamed of it. I like that language too, man. It's way better than English to say what you feel. But German is the best. It's got a real rugged sound, and I'm going to learn to talk it someday.

After Chato I write "de Shamrock." That's the street where I live, and it's the name of the gang I belong to, but the others are all gone now. Their families had to move away, except Gorilla is in jail and Blackie joined the navy because he liked swimming. But I still have our old arsenal. It's buried under the chickens, and I dig it up when I get bored. There's tire irons and chains and pick handles with spikes and two zip guns we made and they shoot real bullets but not very straight. In the good old days nobody cared to tangle with us. But now I'm the only one left.

Well, today started off like any other day. The toilet roars like a hot rod taking off. My father coughs and spits about nineteen times and hollers it's six-thirty. So I holler back I'm quitting school. Things hit me like that — sudden.

"Don't you want to be a lawyer no more," he says in Spanish, "and defend the Mexican people?"

My father thinks he is very funny, and next time I make any plans, he's sure not going to hear about it.

"Don't you want to be a doctor," he says, "and cut off my leg for nothing someday?"

"*Due beast ine dumb cop,*"[1] I tell him in German, but not very loud.

"How will you support me," he says, "when I retire? Or will you marry a rich old woman that owns a pool hall?"

"I'm checking out of this dump! You'll never see me again!"

I hollered it at him, but already he was in the kitchen making a big noise in his coffee. I could be dead and he wouldn't take me serious. So I laid there and waited for him to go off to work. When I woke up again, it was way past eleven. I can sleep forever these days. So I got out of bed and put on clean jeans and my windbreaker and combed myself very neat, because already I had a feeling this was going to be a big day for me.

I had to wait for breakfast because the baby was sick and throwing up milk on everything. There is always a baby vomiting in my house. When they're born, everybody comes over and says: "Qué cute!"[2] but nobody passes any comments on the dirty way babies act. Sometimes my mother asks me to hold one for her but it always cries, maybe because I squeeze it a little hard when nobody's looking.

When my mother finally served me, I had to hold my breath, she smelled so bad of babies. I don't care to look at her anymore. Her legs got those dark-blue rivers running all over them. I kept waiting for her to bawl me out about school, but I guess she forgot, or something. So I cut out.

1 *"Due . . . cop."* "You're an idiot" *("Du bist ein Dummkopf")*.
2 *Qué* how

Every time I go out my front door I have to cry for what they've done to old Shamrock Street. It used to be so fine, with solid homes on both sides. Maybe they needed a little paint here and there but they were cozy. Then the S.P. Railroad bought up all the land except my father's place, because he was stubborn. They came in with their wrecking bars and their bulldozers. You could hear those houses scream when they ripped them down. So now Shamrock Street is just front walks that lead to a hole in the ground, and piles of busted cement. And Pelón's house and Blackie's are just stacks of old boards waiting to get hauled away. I hope that never happens to your street, man.

My first stop was the front gate and there was that sign again, that big S wrapped around a cross like a snake with rays coming out, which is the mark of the Sierra Street gang, as everybody knows. I rubbed it off, but tonight they'll put it back again. In the old days they wouldn't dare to come on our street, but without your gang you're nobody. And one of these fine days they're going to catch up with me in person and that will be the end of Chato de Shamrock.

So I cruised on down to Main Street like a ghost in a graveyard. Just to prove I'm alive, I wrote my name on the fence at the corner. A lot of names you see in public places are written very sloppy. Not me. I take my time. Like my fifth-grade teacher used to say, if other people are going to see your work, you owe it to yourself to do it right. Mrs. Cully was her name and she was real nice, for an Anglo. My other teachers were all cops, but Mrs. Cully drove me home one time when some guys were after me. I think she wanted to adopt me but she never said anything about it. I owe a lot to that lady, and especially my writing. You should see it, man — it's real smooth and mellow, and curvy like a blond in a bikini. Everybody says so. Except one time they had me in Juvenile by mistake and some doctor looked at it. He said it proved I had something wrong with me, some long word. That doctor was crazy, because I made him show me his writing and it was real ugly like a barbwire fence with little chickens stuck on the points. You couldn't even read it.

Anyway, I signed myself very clean and neat on that corner. And then I thought, Why not look for a job someplace? But I was more in the mood to write my name, so I went into the dime store and helped myself to two boxes of crayons and some chalk and cruised on down Main, writing all the way. I wondered should I write more than my name. Should I write "Chato is a fine guy" or "Chato is wanted by the police"? Things like that. News. But I decided against it. Better to keep them guessing. Then I crossed over to Forney Playground. It used to be our territory, but now the Sierra have taken over there like everyplace else. Just to show them, I wrote on the tennis court and the swimming pool and the gym. I left a fine little trail of Chato de Shamrock in eight colors. Some places I used chalk, which works better on brick or plaster. But crayons are the thing for cement or anything smooth, like in the girls' rest room. On that wall I drew a phone number. I bet a lot of them are going to call that number, but it isn't mine because we don't have a phone in the first place, and in the second place I'm probably never going home again.

I'm telling you, I was pretty famous at the Forney by the time I cut out, and from there I continued my travels till something hit me. You know how you put your name on something and that proves it belongs to you? Things like school books or gym shoes? So I thought, How about that, now? And I put my name on the Triple A Market and on Morrie's Liquor Store and on the Zócalo, which is a beer joint. And then I cruised on up Broadway, getting rich. I took over a barber shop and a furniture store and the Plymouth agency. And the firehouse for laughs, and the phone company so I could call all my girl friends and keep my dimes. And then there I was at Webster and García's Funeral Home with the big white columns. At first I thought that might be bad luck, but then I said, Oh, well, we all got to die sometime. So I signed myself, and now I can eat good and live in style and have a big time all my life, and then kiss you all good-bye and give myself the best funeral in L.A. for free.

And speaking of funerals, along came the Sierra right then, eight or ten of them down the street with that stupid walk which is their trademark. I ducked into the garage and hid behind the hearse. Not that I'm a coward. Getting stomped doesn't bother me, or even shot. What I hate is those blades, man. They're like a piece of ice cutting into your belly. But the Sierra didn't see me and went on by. I couldn't hear what they were saying, but I knew they had me on their mind. So I cut on over to the Boys' Club, where they don't let anybody get you, no matter who you are. To pass the time I shot some baskets and played a little pool and watched the television, but the story was boring, so it came to me: Why not write my name on the screen? Which I did with a squeaky pen. Those cowboys sure looked fine with Chato de Shamrock written all over them. Everybody got a kick out of it. But of course up comes Mr. Calderón and makes me wipe it off. They're always spying on you up there. And he takes me into his office and closes the door.

"Well," he says, "and how is the last of the dinosaurs?"

Meaning that the Shamrocks are as dead as giant lizards.

Then he goes into that voice with the church music in it, and I look out of the window.

"I know it's hard to lose your gang, Chato," he says, "but this is your chance to make new friends and straighten yourself out. Why don't you start coming to Boys' Club more?"

"It's boring here," I tell him.

"What about school?"

"I can't go," I said. "They'll get me."

"The Sierra's forgotten you're alive," he tells me.

"Then how come they put their mark on my house every night?"

"Do they?"

He stares at me very hard. I hate those eyes of his. He thinks he knows everything. And what is he? Just a Mexican like everybody else.

"Maybe you put that mark there yourself," he says. "To make yourself big. Just like you wrote on the television."

"That was my name! I like to write my name!"

"So do dogs," he says. "On every lamppost they come to."

"You're a dog yourself," I told him, but I don't think he heard me. He just went on talking. Brother, how they love to talk up there! But I didn't bother to listen, and when he ran out of gas I left. From now on I'm scratching that Boys' Club off my list.

Out on the street it was getting dark, but I could still follow my trail back toward Broadway. It felt good seeing Chato written everyplace, but at the Zócalo I stopped dead. Around my name there was a big red heart done in lipstick with some initials I didn't recognize. To tell the truth, I didn't know how to feel. In one way I was mad that anyone would fool with my name, especially if it was some guy doing it for laughs. But what guy carries lipstick? And if it was a girl, that could be kind of interesting.

A girl is what it turned out to be. I caught up with her at the telephone company. There she is, standing in the shadows, drawing her heart around my name. And she has a very pretty shape on her, too. I sneak up behind her very quiet, thinking all kinds of crazy things and my blood shooting around so fast it shakes me all over. And then she turns around and it's only Crusader Rabbit. That's what we called her from the television show they had then, on account of her teeth in front.

When she sees me, she takes off down the alley, but in twenty feet I catch her. I grab for the lipstick, but she whips it behind her. I reach around and try to pull her fingers open, but her hand is sweaty and so is mine. And there we are, stuck together all the way down. She twists up against me, kind of giggling. To tell the truth, I don't like to wrestle with girls. They don't fight fair. And then we lost balance and fell against some garbage cans, so I woke up. After that I got the lipstick away from her very easy.

"What right you got to my name?" I tell her. "I never gave you permission."

"You sign yourself real fine," she says.

I knew that already.

"Let's go writing together," she says.

"The Sierra's after me."

"I don't care," she says. "Come on, Chato — you and me can have a lot of fun."

She came up close and giggled that way. She put her hand on my hand that had the lipstick in it. And you know what? I'm ashamed to say I almost told her yes. It would be a change to go writing with a girl. We could talk there in the dark. We could decide on the best places. And her handwriting wasn't too bad either. But then I remembered I had my reputation to think of. Somebody would be sure to see us, and they'd be laughing at me all over the Eastside. So I pulled my hand away and told her off.

"Run along, Crusader," I told her. "I don't want no partners, and especially not you."

"Who are you calling Crusader?" she screamed. "You ugly, squash-nose punk."

She called me everything. And spit at my face but missed. I didn't argue. I just cut out. And when I got to the first sewer I threw away her lipstick. Then I drifted over to the banks at Broadway and Bailey, which is a good spot for writing because a lot of people pass by there.

Well, I hate to brag, but that was the best work I've ever done in all my life. Under the street lamp my name shone like solid gold. I stood to one side and checked the people as they walked past and inspected it. With some you can't tell just how they feel, but with others it rings out like a cash register. There was one man. He got out of his Cadillac to buy a paper and when he saw my name he smiled. He was the age to be my father. I bet he'd give me a job if I asked him. I bet he'd take me to his home and to his office in the morning. Pretty soon I'd be sitting at my own desk and signing my name on letters and checks and things. But I would never buy a Cadillac, man. They burn too much gas.

Later a girl came by. She was around eighteen, I think, with green eyes. Her face was so pretty I didn't dare to look at her shape. Do you want me to go crazy? That girl stopped and really studied my name like she fell in love with it. She wanted to know me, I could tell. She wanted to take my hand and we'd go off together holding hands. We'd go to Beverly Hills and nobody would look at us the wrong way. I almost said "Hi" to that girl and, "How do you like my writing?" But not quite.

So here I am, standing on this corner with my chalk all gone and only one crayon left and it's ugly brown. My fingers are too cold besides. But I don't care because I just had a vision, man. Did they ever turn on the lights for you so you could see the whole world and everything in it? That's how it came to me right now. I don't need to be a movie star or boxing champ to make my name in the world. All I need is plenty of chalk and crayons. And that's easy. L.A. is a big city, man, but give me a couple of months and I'll be famous all over town. Of course they'll try to stop me — the Sierra, the police, and everybody. But I'll be like a ghost, man. I'll be real mysterious, and all they'll know is just my name, signed like I always sign it, CHATO DE SHAMROCK with rays shooting out like from the Holy Cross.

George Meneses

Chavalo Encanicado

The author tells this story in the form of a letter by a "chavalo encanicado" — lovestruck youth — known to his friends as el Chapo. Through his use of language and his selection of details, George Meneses has created an entertaining tale that reveals a lighthearted side of barrio life. "Chavalo Encanicado" first appeared in the Los Angeles barrio magazine Con Safos, *on whose editorial staff he served. Meneses is vice-principal of a southern California high school.*

Mira[1] Rafas,

I started telling you about my cousin Tudi the last time I was in Los. Since I didn't finish the story, I'll just write you a short letter. I'll tell you how it was en nuestros tiempos, ése.[2]

The cold lights of Los seen from my house in the barrio were not warm like my house and my family, ése. We always were taught to love life — in the way we laughed, in the way we danced, and in the way we enjoyed everything. But one kind of life we always had, more than any other kind, was chickens. ¡Hijo! [3] Sometimes the other kids couldn't play tag in my yard for tripping on the chickens. Sure there was a dog, a goat, some rabbits, but always we had more chickens than anything.

Nicky Porras had a poultry shop, and every month I had to kill and pluck about thirty chickens for my mother, who sold them to Nicky. Life was good for me then except for all them chickens. Those chickens almost messed up my love life for good, ése.

Rachel and Virgie were sisters, and man, were they

1 *Mira* Look
2 *en . . . ése* back in our time, man
3 *¡Hijo!* Son (of a)!

fine. They weren't really, but they looked like twins. They had eyes that were black and bright like the buttons on my mother's blue dress. Rachel always had little gold earrings that looked like crosses and Virgie always had ribbons in her hair. Red ribbons, blue ribbons, or green ribbons. And always the vatos[4] would wait every day to see what color ribbons Virgie would wear that day. It was a guessing game about Virgie's ribbons.

My cousin Tudi and me had tried to take out those chicks, but always it was the same. They couldn't go out, or the mother was sick, or they were going to their aunt's house in T.J.[5] When I saw Rachel, my heart would beat fast and my mouth would get dry. My sister Lucía would call me sinvergüenza.[6] I guess Lucía was right. I was the roughest vato in the barrio, except maybe for Half-Man, and I was so encanicado with Rachel that it would hurt inside my heart when I saw her going to the store or hanging clothes in the back yard. Tudi dug Virgie but it wasn't the same. Era muy cold-blooded, mi primo Tudi.[7]

One Saturday we was hunting doves out of season in San Fernando and me and Tudi were feeling all warm inside. The little bit of Red Mountain wine that old Alfredo had bought us was working good. Really fine. But the warm thing was not only in the wine. Warmness came too because me and Tudi had finally made a date with Rachel and Virgie, and man, we couldn't think of nothing else.

We couldn't go to their house to pick them up 'cause their old man didn't dig on vatos taking out his daughters. Me and Tudi didn't argue. Their father wasn't called Big Bad Joe Garza for nothing. I ain't no fool, ése. Tudi neither.

We carried our .22s as we crossed the big field in San Fernando. We like to go up there to hunt the doves. Man, it was a hot sun. But it was a good hot sun. Someday, I thought, I'm going to learn to whistle like that bird on the

4 *vatos* guys; dudes (pachuco slang)
5 *T.J.* Tijuana, Mexico
6 *sinvergüenza* scoundrel (literally, "shameless one")
7 *Era . . . Tudi.* He was very cold-blooded, my cousin Tudi.

fence. That bird don't care that me and Tudi are walking toward him. He wants to sing, and he don't care about no Mexicans with .22s.

We sat under a bush to rest. We listened to the small animal noises that was all around us. ¡Qué vida! [8] We talked about tonight when we would be at Lourdes Hall doing a slow rock with Rachel and Virgie. The date was to meet them at the hall in back of Our Lady of Lourdes Church. Everything was set. Tudi was going to borrow his tío[9] Poncho's car. When we got back to Los, we would take a good bath and make it to the dance. Life is really good when you got a little wine, a good day for hunting doves, a chance to use a car, and a date with the two finest chicks in the barrio. ¡Ay, que si estaban buenas! [10]

My cousin Tudi lived across the street from my house. Besides Tudi, my tía[11] Chelo had cousins Neto and Fina and a big white dog named Chico what bites tin cans and rocks for to keep his teeth sharp. And man, did that dog keep them sharp!

Later that afternoon, cuando llegamos bien prendidos,[12] I went in my house knowing that Tudi would call me when it was time for the dance. I had only two doves, and I gave them to my mother. I didn't tell her that Tudi had shot both of them. So what if I was a lousy shot. Tonight — my heart began to beat really fast. I made myself lighten up. Right now I was hungry, so I rolled myself some cold beans in a tortilla and sat outside on the old car seat under the fig tree, contemplando las moscas[13] that gather because of the chickens.

Having finished my refín,[14] I went to take my bath to get ready. And then was when my mother let all of the roof of the world fall on my head. She told me that Nicky Porras was coming for the chickens at seven o'clock.

8 *¡Qué vida!* What a life!
9 *tío* uncle
10 *¡Ay . . . buenas!* Wow, were they ever fine!
11 *tía* aunt
12 *cuando . . . prendidos* when we arrived well lit (under the influence of alcohol)
13 *contemplando las moscas* gazing at the flies
14 *refín* meal (pachuco slang)

Me with a date in less than two hours and thirty-two chickens to clean and pluck! Me lleva a la[15] . . . wait! . . . "Tudi!" Man, I went running out of the house yelling, "Tudi! . . . the chickens . . . Tudi!"

My tía Chelo came running out of the house, muy apurada,[16] like when I fell and broke my arm. "¿Qué pasa?" [17] she asked me.

"What happened?" Me lleva a la . . . "I got thirty-two chickens to kill, that's what happened!"

My tía then said, con aquella paciencia, "¡Ay Chapito, cómo eres escandaloso!" [18]

"¿Escandaloso?" Me, with the chance of a lifetime vanishing in a bad dream of chicken blood and feathers; and she says que soy[19] escandaloso. Trouble is, some people don't really know what gets to be important in a growing vato's life.

Anyways, Tudi comes running out. "Relax, ése," he said, "we'll get it done in time."

When I think back to that time, it almost makes me sick because of what happened after that. First Tudi said to use my father's hatchet. It was very sharp for killing chickens. We tried to do it like an assembly line. I held the chicken and Tudi cut the neck. Only he missed. Man, he cut that chicken on the chest and it went running, squirting blood, and screaming like it was dying or something.

After that, we put a big bote to boil with water to soften the feathers for plucking. We put it on a fire made with sticks. Then we put the dead chickens in the water. Only some of the chickens wasn't dead. I complained, "Tudi, some of those chickens aren't dead, ése!"

"So what?" Tudi said. "They're going to die anyway, ése!" Mi primo Tudi es muy gacho.[20]

15 *Me lleva a la* Well, I'll be a
16 *muy apurada* hurriedly
17 *"¿Qué pasa?"* "What's going on?"
18 *con . . . escandaloso!* with that patience of hers, "Oh Chapito, you're so excitable!"
19 *que soy* that I am
20 *Mi . . . gacho.* My cousin is quite cruel.

Then there was smoke and fire and scared chickens; there was blood on my hair, feathers in my mouth, and Tudi screaming at me, "Chapo! Hold that chicken! I almost cut my hand, loco!"

Then we gave up with the dangerous hatchet. Next we were pulling their heads off by giving them the big twist in the air. The chickens would go flip-flopping all over the yard. Even the goat was covered with blood! I yelled at Tudi, "Orale,[21] loco, you threw that chicken on the clothesline."

But Tudi didn't listen. His eyes were shiny and wide open. His face is sweating and he keeps on saying, "Hurry, Chapo, hurry!" I ran to get another chicken. I tell you, Rafas, it was like the Three Stooges, but there was only two, me and Tudi.

By the time we got to chicken number thirty-two, my arms hurt like the time we mixed cement for the basement. My head hurt and I'm for throwing up from the feathers and the blood. But we got them plucked. Each one, loco.

Now for a good bath and the dance. We are wiping off the feathers when Joey, what is Rachel and Virgie's little brother, comes in the yard. Joey is maybe a little bit chiple[22] but he is good for bringing us messages from his sisters. I got a bad feeling about what he was going to tell us. He stopped and looked around at the feathers and the blood; then he smiled. Man, I don't like that smile. He started to giggle. "My father," said Joey, "says that because my cousin Sophie is fat from a baby, my sisters can't go to no dances."

¡Qué gacho! [23] Sophie gets pansona and Virgie and Rachel can't go to the dance. That ain't right, loco. Everything happens to me. The chickens get plucked but no dance, no Rachel, no nothing. Tudi don't care. He went to the dance anyway. I don't feel like doing nothing. That Tudi, what a vato. Any babe is okay for him. Me? My mother is mad 'cause we only had twenty-nine chickens

21 *"Orale"* "Hey, c'mon"
22 *chiple* pampered; spoiled
23 *¡Qué gacho!* What a drag!

for Nicky. Two looked too ugly from the cuts on the chest, and one got left in the water too long and was almost cooked.

The warmth from my heart is gone. The warmth from my house and family is gone. Only the cold lights from the city below the barrio are left; the cold lights and the cold, dead chickens.

Well, Rafas, that's the way it was. That night my mother fixed pollo en mole[24] for dinner, but I wasn't too hungry. . . . Tú sabes. . . . A'i te watcho, vato.[25] I don't feel too good.

Tu camarada,[26]
El Chapo
c/s

24 *pollo en mole* chicken dish with a special chile sauce
25 *Tú sabes . . . vato.* You know. . . . See ya later, dude.
26 *Tu camarada* Your buddy

ROLANDO R. HINOJOSA-S.

My Aunt Panchita

Likely to be found in the typical barrio, north or south, is a local curandera or curandero: a folk healer. In this second sketch from his prize-winning Estampas del Valle/Sketches of the Valley, *Hinojosa tells of the day when a curandera was called in to cure Rafael Buenrostro, who first appeared on page 9. The author, who has taught at New Mexico Highlands and other universities, now serves as a dean at Texas A & I University at Kingsville.*

"Where's the patient?"

"Right here, Aunt Panchita; come in, please."

"Ah, so it's Rafa. . . . What's wrong with you, child?"

"We don't know; yesterday he began to stammer and now there he is, shaking with fever."

"Okay, close the curtains. Everybody out and close the door behind you, I'm gonna begin."

Aunt Panchita took out a brownish egg from the grocery bag and made the sign of the cross with it over Rafa Buenrostro's face. Then she made another sign of the cross covering his entire body and began to pray:

"Prayer and incantation to drive away fright: Child of God, I heal you by incantation in the name of God and the Holy Spirit. Three distinct persons and one true God. Saint Roque, Saint Sebastian, eleven thousand virgins: by your most glorious passion and ascension, deign to heal this child afflicted with the evil eye, fright, fever, or any other malady not dealt with by you or by your sacrosanct mystery. Jesus, Son of God, remember your God. How loving is Jesus, how loving is Jesus, world without end, amen.

"Offering. Jesus be your doctor, Most Holy Mary be your doctor, and may this sickness be dispelled through the love of God, through the love of God, amen."

Aunt Panchita repeated the prayer, the incantation, and the offering twice, then broke the egg in a green plate, which she placed under the bed. Rafa Buenrostro breathed deeply and fell into a sleep that lasted a day and a half.

Aunt Panchita left hurriedly, saying that she'd be back on Wednesday. Being a very busy woman, Aunt Panchita was on her way to the baptism of Lino Carrizales' child.

RICARDO SÁNCHEZ

i yearn

Perhaps because he has reflected on his experiences in the El Paso barrio from several distant and distinct vantage points, Ricardo Sánchez has been able to re-create with accuracy and sensitivity the "feeling" of barrio life. Few writers have been able to convey the essence of a barrio so successfully. The caló he refers to is the Spanish-English originally spoken by the pachuco (pages 28 and 56) — the distinctive speech that has contributed to the language spoken by most Chicanos today.

i yearn this morning
what i've yearned
since i left

    almost a year ago . . .

it is hollow
this
being away
from everyday life
in the barrios
of my homeland . . .
all those cities
like el paso, los angeles,
albuquerque,
denver, san antonio
    (off into chicano
            infinitum!);

i yearn
to hear spanish
spoken in caló —

that special way
chicanos roll their
  tongues
to form
words
which dart or glide;

i yearn
for foods
that have character
and strength — the kind
that assail yet caress
you with the zest of life;

more than anything,
i yearn, my people,
for the warmth of you
greeting me with "¿qué tal,
hermano?" [1]
and the knowing that you
  mean it
when you tell me that you love
the fact that we exist. . . .

1 *"¿qué tal, hermano?"* "how goes it, brother?"

La Chicana

The Chicana Woman

When women speak,
the community listens.

Marta Cotera

Rodriguez S.F.
© '75

FABIOLA CABEZA DE BACA

The Women of New Mexico

A member of an old and highly respected New Mexico family, Fabiola Cabeza de Baca tells of the history of her state as she learned about it and as she herself lived it. In this section of We Fed Them Cactus, *published in 1954, she focuses on the role that the women in her family — and other women like them — played in this history. The Llano to which she refers is the rolling plains country in the southeastern part of the state, where Ceja is located. La Liendre is in the higher country farther north, near Las Vegas, New Mexico.*

The women on the Llano and Ceja played a great part in the history of the land. It was a difficult life for a woman, but she had made her choice when in the marriage ceremony she had promised to obey and to follow her husband. It may not have been her choice, since parents may have decided for her. It was the Spanish custom to make matches for the children. Whether through choice or tradition, the women had to be a hardy lot in order to survive the long trips by wagon or carriage and the separation from their families, if their families were not among those who were settling on the Llano.

The women had to be versed in the curative powers of plants and in midwifery, for there were no doctors within a radius of two hundred miles or more.

The knowledge of plant medicine is an inheritance from the Moors, and brought to New Mexico by the first Spanish colonizers. From childhood we are taught the names of herbs, weeds, and plants that have curative potency; even today, when we have doctors at our immediate call, we still have great faith in plant medicine. Certainly this knowledge of home remedies was a source of comfort to the women who went out to the Llano, yet their faith in God helped more than anything in their survival.

Every village had its curandera or médica, and the ranchers rode many miles to bring the medicine woman or the midwife from a distant village or neighboring ranch.

Quite often the wife of the patrón was well versed in plant medicine. I know that my grandmother, doña Estéfana Delgado de Baca, although not given the name of médica, because it was not considered proper in her social class, was called every day by some family in the village, or by their empleados, to treat a child or some other person in the family. In the fall of the year she went out to the hills and valleys to gather her supply of healing herbs. When she went to live in La Liendre, there were terrible outbreaks of smallpox and she had difficulty convincing the villagers that vaccination was a solution. Not until she had a godchild in every family was she able to control the dreaded disease. In Spanish tradition a godmother takes the responsibility of a real mother, and in that way grandmother conquered many superstitions which the people had. At least she had the power to decide what should be done for her godchildren.

From El Paso, Texas, she secured vaccines from her cousin Dr. Samaniego. She vaccinated her children, grandchildren, and godchildren against the disease. She vaccinated me when I was three years old, and the vaccination has passed many doctors' inspections.

As did my grandmother, so all the wives of the patrones held a very important place in the villages and ranches on the Llano. The patrón ruled the rancho, but his wife looked after the spiritual and physical welfare of the empleados and their families. She was the first one called when there was death, illness, misfortune, or good tidings in a family. She was a great social force in the community — more so than her husband. She held the purse strings, and thus she was able to do as she pleased in her charitable enterprises and to help those who might seek her assistance.

There may have been class distinction in the larger

towns, but the families on the Llano had none; the empleados and their families were as much a part of the family of the patrón as his own children. It was a very democratic way of life.

The women in these isolated areas had to be resourceful in every way. They were their own doctors, dressmakers, tailors, and advisers.

The settlements were far apart and New Mexico was a poor territory trying to adapt itself to a new rule. The Llano people had no opportunity for public schools before statehood, but there were men and women who held classes for the children of the patrones in private homes. They taught reading in Spanish and sometimes in English. Those who had means sent their children to school in Las Vegas, Santa Fe, or Eastern states. If no teachers were available, the mothers taught their own children to read, and many of the wealthy ranchers had private teachers for their children until they were old enough to go away to boarding schools.

Doña Luisa Gallegos de Baca, who herself had been educated in a convent in the Middle West, served as teacher to many of the children on the Llano territory.

Without the guidance and comfort of the wives and mothers, life on the Llano would have been unbearable, and a great debt is owed to the brave pioneer women who ventured into the cruel life of the plains, far from contact with the outside world. Most of them have gone to their eternal rest, and God must have saved a very special place for them to recompense them for their contribution to colonization and religion in an almost savage country.

LEONARD ADAMÉ

My Grandmother Would Rock Quietly and Hum

Although Leonard Adamé comes from the San Joaquin Valley of California, his memories of his grandmother might easily be those of Chicano men and women from Chicago, San Antonio, or Tucson. In stanzas of very short lines he creates a portrait of his grandmother — what she did, the way she looked, and the way she made him feel. The reader not only encounters another person but is able — to an unusual degree — to share the poet's feeling for that person.

in her house
she would rock quietly and hum
until her swelled hands
calmed

in summer
she wore thick stockings
sweaters
and gray braids

(when el cheque came
we went to Payless
and I laughed greedily
when given a quarter)

mornings,
sunlight barely lit
the kitchen
and where
there were shadows
it was not cold

she quietly rolled
flour tortillas —

the papas[1]
cracking in hot lard
would wake me

she had lost her teeth
and when we ate
she had bread
soaked in café

always her eyes
were clear
and she could see
as I cannot yet see —
through her eyes
she gave me herself

she would sit
and talk
of her girlhood —
of things strange to me:
  México
  epidemics
  relatives shot
  her father's hopes
  of this country —
how they sank
with cement dust
to his insides

now
when I go
to the old house
the worn spots
by the stove
echo of her shuffling
and
México
still hangs in her
fading
calendar pictures

1 *papas* potatoes

Tomás Rivera

A Prayer

The varied experiences of Chicanos are dramatized in Tomás Rivera's notable collection of short stories, ...y no se lo tragó la tierra/...and the earth did not part. *Each story is preceded by a short anecdote which in some way relates to it. This anecdote and story center around a mother's concern about a soldier son. By writing his story in the form of a mother's prayer, the author has given his subject matter unusual poignance. Tomás Rivera is a dean at the University of Texas at San Antonio.*

She had fallen asleep immediately, and all of them, being very careful not to cross their arms, nor their legs, nor their hands, looked at her intently. His spirit was already in her body.

"Let's see, what can I do for you tonight, brothers?"

"Well, you see, I haven't heard from my son for almost two months. Yesterday I received a letter from the government saying that he was lost in action. I would like to know if he's alive or not. It's driving me crazy just thinking and thinking about it."

"Don't worry, sister. Julianito is all right. He's all right. Don't worry about him. He'll be in your arms soon. He'll be back next month."

"Thank you. Thank you very much."

God, Jesus Christ, most holy in my heart, this is the third Sunday that I've come to pray, to beg of you to bring me news of my son. I haven't heard from him. Protect him, dear God, that a bullet will not pierce his heart like doña Virginia's son, may he rest in peace. Take care of him for me, Jesus, protect him from the bullets, take pity on him; he's a good boy. Ever since he was a baby and I would put him to sleep while nursing him he was a good boy, very appreciative; he never bit me. He's very innocent, protect him, he doesn't want to harm anyone; he's of noble spirit; he is very kind; don't let a bullet pierce his heart.

Please, Virgin Mary, you protect him, too. Shelter his body, cover his head, blind the Communists' eyes, the Koreans' and the Chinese's so that they won't see him, so they won't kill him. I'm still keeping his childhood toys, his cars, his trucks, even a kite I found the other day in the closet. And also the postcards and the comics from the time he began to read. I'm keeping everything for when he returns.

Protect him, Jesus, don't let them kill him. I've always promised a visit to La Virgen de San Juan and also to La Virgen de Guadalupe. He has a medal of La Virgen de San Juan del Valle and he also made a vow; he wants to live.

Take care of him, cover his heart with your hand so that no bullet can penetrate it. He's a kind boy. He was afraid to go; he told me so. The day that they took him, when he said farewell to me, he embraced me and cried for a little while. I felt his heart beat and I remembered when he was a baby and I nursed him, and how happy we both were.

Please take care of him, I beg of you. I promise you my life for his. Bring him home safe and sound from Korea.

Protect his heart with your hands. Jesus, Holy Father, Virgen de Guadalupe, give me back his life, bring me back his heart. Why have they taken him? He hasn't done anything. He doesn't know anything. He's very humble. He doesn't want to take anyone's life. Bring him back alive; I don't want him dead.

I offer you my heart for his. Here it is. I offer you my throbbing heart; if you want blood, tear it from me, tear it out of me. I give it to you in exchange for my son's. Here it is. Here is my heart! . . . My heart has his very own blood. . . .

Bring him back alive to me and I shall give up my heart to you.

RICHARD VÁSQUEZ

Angelina Sandoval

Published in 1970, the novel Chicano *recounts the experiences of four generations of the Sandoval family in California. This excerpt from* Chicano *focuses on the oldest member of the second generation of Sandovals to be born in the United States. In Angelina Sandoval the reader not only meets a dynamic young woman but is introduced to the difficulties that a spirited member of her generation would have faced. This part of the novel takes place during World War II and the years prior to it. The author of* Chicano *once was a construction worker but is now a professional writer who lives near Los Angeles.*

Angelina Sandoval was the eldest offspring of don Neftalí and doña Alicia Sandoval. Her first impression of the world around her had been negative. When she was a toddler, her parents made no attempt to hide their disappointment at her being born a girl. The oldest child, she came to realize, should always be a boy. When the first-born was a girl, a little awkwardness was involved in overlooking her and bypassing her in favor of the first boy to be born in the family.

Thank God, don Neftalí and doña Alicia thought when their second child was a boy. Now, regardless of the sex or number of subsequent progeny, the family pattern could commence. The eldest son would be second in command in the family. He would be consulted (and only he) concerning any plans regarding building, moving, or the acquisition of anything material. He would inherit, regardless of the needs of any of the other siblings. If the family could afford only one education, or only one of anything advantageous, it would be his. This was a custom, a way of life which the family accepted without question — except when a girl was born first. Then the family accepted this way of life and this custom with a tiny bit of question.

Augmenting the awkwardness of the situation were several things. First, Angelina was a very bright child and had to go to school in the nearby Anglo community. Within a few years she was speaking and reading English, and she learned that the rest of the world didn't feel about firstborn sons and daughters the way her parents felt. Her first reaction was that she had been cheated by being a girl. Her second was that the subsequent children had been cheated by having an elder brother. Another reaction was that her younger brother, who was the older brother, was extremely selfish in thinking that things were fine just as they were.

One morning when Angelina was about eight years old, and Gregorio was seven, and Victorio was six, and Luisa was five, and Orlando was four, and little Pedro was three, and Roberto, Rita, and Delores were not born yet, the family was seated at the table having breakfast.

Little Pedro squealed in delight as he shoved a handful of beans into his mouth. Angelina took a large square white cloth that had been a flour sack, now used as a napkin by all the children in turn, and wiped the bean-and-potato-streaked face of her youngest brother. Through eating, Papa Sandoval sat finishing his coffee, rolling a cigarette, regarding first Angelina and then the family pride, the oldest son, Gregorio.

"Too bad," he said to his wife for the hundredth time, "that she had to be so light and he so dark."

Doña Alicia looked for the ten millionth time at the dark, homely, Indianlike face of her oldest son. It almost seemed to her that Gregorio's face became a shade darker at hearing his father's words. The boy was looking intently at Angelina.

"Yes," the mother said, as she had so many times before, "had he been born first, he would have had the light skin."

Angelina found herself returning Gregorio's stare. She knew the parents' words did not hurt him, only reminded him. It was at school. The Anglo kids. How they taunted him, left him out. There were many other Mexican children at the school, but only a few were as dark, squat-featured, and . . . non-Anglo-looking — she realized — as her brother. She had many times examined herself in the piece of broken mirror above the stone sink. Her olive skin (lighter, actually), black hair, black eyes with a tiny bit of what looked like smoke in the whites, her features — all combined to make her look Mexican, to be sure, but very unlike Gregorio. The other Sandoval children varied in appearance between the relative extremes of Angelina and Gregorio.

Now the other children looked at the two older ones, then began screaming at their mother, "Mama! How light am I?" "I'm lighter than you!" "Look here, Mama," said Victorio, showing the untanned underside of his arm.

By virtue of the futility of the situation Angelina felt but little sympathy for Gregorio. She remembered his severe rebuff when, in the unintentionally cruel way of children, the Anglo kids let Gregorio know his being the oldest son meant nothing to them. Well she could understand his dislike at leaving this little community whenever it was necessary, where being the eldest son entitled him to accompany his father on adult business to other homes where his position in the family was recognized as an important one. But Angelina had heard even the friendliest, most well-intentioned of neighbors in Irwindale say, "Too bad he's so dark. Poor thing."

At the age of sixteen Angelina was told by her father to stay out of school and work in a nearby packinghouse to help support the family. Gregorio, a year younger, stayed in school. "It's necessary that he prepare himself," the old man said, but Angelina never did quite understand what he was to prepare himself for. Then when Victorio was sixteen, he also went to work beside his father in the fields, and the following year when Rosita was sixteen, she too went to work.

Don Neftalí's plan was to get Gregorio started in a little cobbler shop. While modernization had defeated Neftalí on different occasions in the past, "People will always need shoes," he told his family. And it was necessary that

Gregorio get all the schooling he can, so that he might be a successful businessman. There was an old, old man, so old he could remember the gringos arriving around Rabbit Town in covered wagons, and he had been a zapatero, a cobbler. Neftalí invited him to the house, and the three of them — Neftalí, the old man, and Gregorio — made plans. They would build a little shop next to the house. With the money the older children earned, Neftalí would buy the necessary equipment and pay the old man — Pelón, Baldy, he was called — to teach Gregorio the cobbling trade. And within a few months Gregorio drove a large stake into the ground in front of the house and nailed a hand-lettered sign reading ZAPATERO across it.

But the year was 1941. The family for years had had delivered a daily English-language newspaper. Now the children read to Neftalí, translating into Spanish the news, and explaining why all the boys over eighteen had to register for the draft. Pedro was just eighteen and Gregorio was twenty-two years old, and Victorio and Orlando were in between. Together, Gregorio assuming leadership, they went to the nearest town to register, and within weeks they were all told to report for induction, except for Orlando, who was retarded. Neftalí and Alicia had recognized his affliction and taken him out of school early, dubbed him Poca Luz,[1] and had him work in the fields. To them he could be as useful as anyone else, even if the gringo schools didn't want him.

The war dragged on. The three boys came home several times, rarely together. Neftalí noticed they were changing. With the exception of Gregorio, they seemed only to tolerate the family system and traditions of Neftalí and their mother, Alicia. "I bought a stitching machine," Neftalí proudly told them. "When Gregorio returns for good, he'll have a fine business."

On a hot, dusty afternoon as Angelina arrived home from the packing plant she found a Western Union messenger trying to make her mother and father understand they were to accept and sign for a telegram. She signed

1 *Poca Luz* Scant Light

and thanked the messenger, then turned to her wide-eyed parents. She had already seen it was from the War Department. A chilling lump formed in her stomach as she kept her face calm and opened the envelope. *Which one?*

She read the brief sentences with hardly more than a glance and then said softly, "It's a death notice, Papa."

Neftalí's face grew taut and white, and Alicia's head began shaking as her face screwed up. "Which one?" Neftalí asked, trembling. "Not Gregorio, I know."

Angelina knew there was no kind, pleasant way.

"Yes, Gregorio has been killed." She felt as though she was in a trance as she saw her father stiffen and her mother begin tearing her hair and screaming. It was more than an hour later before Neftalí and Alicia could ask for further details, and Angelina gave them what meager information the telegram contained: that Gregorio was buried on a little island in the Pacific, that his belongings would be coming soon. She left them clutching one another and set about to inform her other Army brothers so they might be home for the services.

Pedro and Victorio came home and the family walked to the little stone church a quarter-mile away. After the services the family walked slowly back, through the fields of cactus and sand and boulders, to the stone house Neftalí had built himself.

They sat around the kitchen–living room, the Sandoval family, now reduced to ten members. Pedro and Victorio, still in their immaculate Army uniforms, said nothing. The younger children began warily to play and drift into the added stone rooms. Neftalí and Alicia sat at the dinner table, palms to their foreheads, stifling sobs.

Victorio, now the eldest son, broke the silence.

"Papa, I can take over the cobbler shop. Perhaps not as well as Gregorio could have, but I can turn it into a thriving business, once I'm out of the Army. I know I can. . . ."

Neftalí shook his head. "No. It wasn't meant to be. There won't be a cobbler shop. I have already made arrangements with Pelón to buy the equipment and supplies. None of you has had the training or preparation to begin a business." And he continued to brood over the death of his eldest son.

They sat. Soon all the younger children were in the other rooms, away from the despair and depression. The older offspring sat self-consciously, occasionally glancing at one another, knowing sooner or later the mood would have to change. The soldiers found themselves looking at Angelina. Somehow her face was different from what it should be. She wore a black dress, almost tight, showing off her well-shaped figure. Her long black hair was smooth and shiny. Her expression was one now of anger and impatience instead of grief. Suddenly she arose, standing straight and tall.

She spoke English, as they all did when they preferred that their parents not understand the conversation. "Well, I've had enough."

She said it simply, with conviction, hands on hips as she faced her brothers. They looked puzzled. The old man looked up from the table, a little annoyed.

"What do you mean?" Victorio asked, his voice low, his attitude still one of remorse.

Angelina looked at each one a moment before continuing. "I mean, when you guys get out of the Army you can come back here and spend the rest of your life picking oranges and using an outside open toilet, but you won't find me here."

Pedro was looking at her evenly, but Victorio seemed angered. "Angie! What are you talking about?"

Neftalí Sandoval raised his voice above the others. "Now listen! I won't have you speaking English in front of your mother and me. We have the right to know. . . ."

Angelina turned to him, speaking politely but firmly. "Please, Papa. Stay out of this. We have something to discuss. When we work it out, we'll tell you about it."

Rarely had a son or daughter talked back to him, but Neftalí knew this was one of the changes coming about in the younger generation raised away from the old country. He remained silent.

Angelina continued. "You, Victorio, are a gutless wonder. You won't say a word about Papa not letting you run a shop. He'd rather give it away than let one of you take Gregorio's place. Well, listen to me. I paid for half that stuff there and helped support Gregorio while he sat learning to drive tacks into soles. I'm twenty-three years old, and you know how many dates I've had? Not one real one, that's how many. Every time a boy came to see me Papa would interview him. Or worse yet — and I truthfully couldn't stand it another time — if Papa wasn't going to be here, he'd appoint Gregorio to look him over. And if he looked like a good prospect for me" — she jerked her thumb — "out he'd go. Because I'm needed to help bring in money."

Victorio was looking shocked. Orlando sat uncertainly, as usual, taking it all in. Pedro, however, was listening intently.

Victorio said, "Angie, all this was for your own good. Dad was raised in the old country. We shouldn't be talking like this about the old traditions. . . ."

"Oh, I'll tell you how sacred the old traditions are. If things had been really tough, he'd have married me off to the first cholo[2] that came along when I was fifteen. But I was able to work all the time. So that makes him extremely selective in my behalf. Now there's not a guy within ten miles who'll come near me, because he'll have to give a personal history to Dad or my brother. I've had it and I'm getting out of here, and if you guys are smart, you won't come back."

Victorio persisted. "But the folks. They need money. Dad makes very little and there's still the younger kids. . . ."

"Good grief, Victor. I could get a factory job in the city, support myself, and still send Mama and Papa more money than I make packing fruit."

"But . . . living by yourself in a city . . . it's not proper for a girl —"

"*Girl!* I'm practically an old maid."

"There'd be none of us to look after you and see that you meet the right boy. . . ."

2 *cholo* a mestizo (of mixed Indian and Spanish blood) peasant of humble origins

Angelina gave a huge shrug and turned her back. "It's hopeless. The way you're talking, I'm more than ever convinced I've got to get out of here. Now. Immediately."

Pedro stood up and spoke for the first time. "She's right, Vic. That's the way I feel, too." He spoke with more of a Spanish accent than the others, and now his voice cracked, as though he was ready to cry. "I'm tired of this way. All my life, I've had the feeling I don't matter to Mama and Papa. I helped pay for Gregorio's shop, also. I'm good enough to work hard in the fields from age sixteen, but not good enough to learn to use the tools I sweated to help buy. Since I've been in the Army I've learned other people don't live like we do. Not even the Mexicanos in the cities. They laugh and say we're Mexican hillbillies."

Orlando sat listening, squinting, concentrating, trying to understand. He remained silent. Neftalí sat glaring, impatiently waiting to be told what the heated conversation was about. Alicia looked bewildered. She too had not understood a word.

Victorio stared at Angelina a few moments, then said, "All right. What do you plan to do?"

She faced him squarely. "Get out of here. Now. Today, quickly, so there's not the slightest chance I'll lose my nerve and reconsider for even a week."

"Where'll you go?"

"The Ornelas family. They live in East Los Angeles. Olivia Ornelas invited me to come and stay there. There's plenty of defense plant work. And I'm going."

They all looked at one another. Neftalí cleared his throat.

"Okay, now tell *them* about it," Victorio said, indicating their parents. Angelina waited a long moment, sighed, then turned to her mother and father still seated at the dinner table.

"Papa, Mama, please try to understand. . . ."

"I don't understand," Neftalí said when she'd finished. "Why? We have it good here. We've always had plenty to eat. So we all do have to work hard. The Bible says — "

"Don't try, Papa," Angelina said softly. "My mind's made up. I'm going to get my things together now."

Neftalí's eyes were watering. "I know this never would have happened in Mexico. It's because you see all the gringos, who have no sense of proper behavior. No one looks after the gringas to see that every man that happens by doesn't take advantage of them. It's because you've seen them in their loose way, that you no longer want to have propriety — "

Angelina pressed her forefinger to his lips gently to shut off the conversation. There were tears in her eyes too as she said, "You're right, Papa."

Pedro coughed once and came to stand in front of his father. "I have to be getting back to camp," he said, a little nervously. "I'll walk with Angelina to the bus stop and leave from there. I'd better be going. The Army is hard on you when you're late." He paused, obviously wanting to say more. Neftalí waited. "And Papa, when I get out in a year or so, I'll come to see you. But don't make plans for me. I have plans of my own."

Neftalí looked at him hard for nearly a minute. Then he slumped a little. "All right, son," he said. He looked at Victorio. "And you? Are you wanting to leave your family, too?"

Victorio looked at the stone floor. "No, Papa. I'll come back to stay."

Neftalí regarded Orlando, still sitting silently on the couch. "And my son with the small light in his brain," he said fondly, "he'll always be with me."

MARTA COTERA

When Women Speak

In this article Marta Cotera responds to those who characterize Chicana feminism as an outgrowth of the women's liberation movement. Her discussion of the Chicana today includes an unusual survey of some heroines of Mexican and Mexican American history. A professional librarian, Marta Cotera is also a Chicana activist and a supporter of the Raza Unida party, to which she refers. La Raza Unida was founded in 1970 by José Angel Gutiérrez in Crystal City, Texas.

All recent literature on Chicanas begins with the trite statement that "the Chicana role is changing its traditional conservative aspects to aggressive feminism," suggesting strong influences of the white women's liberation movement, and suggesting also catastrophic effects on Chicano communities.

Needless to say, such statements have created alarm within our community. Unfortunately often, the persons most affected are Chicanos who have been actively working for the development of women and for the participation of the entire family in Chicano movement activities.

Without the benefit of formal evaluations or in-depth social analysis, Chicana activists can refute the assertion in the first paragraph of this article. The position of Chicanas within our culture may be traditional, but it is not conservative. The so-called changing role is actually a continuing growth process originating with our ancient Indian heritage and moving always toward a stronger position for the woman within our culture. The entire process is consistent with our legacy of Mexicano/Chicano feminism influenced by technological and sociological changes in Chicano areas in the United States and in Mexico. Anglo feminism has had little to do with the development of the Chicana.

The position of the Mexicana in the family structure and community is a dynamic one, calling for a great deal of decision-making, where her opinions and decisions regarding education, child rearing, family expenditures, and politics are taken seriously and seldom overruled or vetoed by any man. Chicano families fluctuate from patriarchy to matriarchy, depending on who survives in the family or the sex of the oldest members. "La Jefita" has an indisputable power position equal to that of "el Jefito," and often decision-making is one hundred percent on her shoulders.

We have the background for using our minds and intellect for the development of the family and the community. In countless cases right now in the American cities the women in our wards, our barrios, our towns are political chieftains, as is the case in Crystal, Texas; Santa Maria, Texas; Austin, Texas.

The only way we have been able to explain this situation to interested Anglos has been to say that Anglo women can move about more freely, but they have been stifled intellectually. Chicanas may not travel from one end of the country to the other, but their minds and intellects have been free. And we see this position as a true indication of liberation, contrary to the stereotypic view of our family life as being traditionally conservative. With this intellectual freedom a Mexicana can continue to move more easily toward a positive, workable, one-to-one relationship with males. In other words, we feel we are progressing from a more advanced state than other women in other cultures toward full development of women.

Research and detailed analysis of our cultural patterns and tradition of strong women prove that we have a long, beautiful history of Mexicano and Chicano feminism which is not Anglo-inspired, imposed, or oriented.

In fact, the entire community should be proud of the feminists in our history. We have a rich legacy of heroines and activists in social movements and armed rebellions, from which we can draw models to emulate. Mexicanas were worshipped as goddesses, honored as queens, and respected as warriors during the pre-Columbian period. During the colonial period, key supporters of the independence movement were women, like doña Josefa Ortiz de Domínguez, the corregidora[1] from Guanajuato. She was only one of many among countless women who supported the cause of independence. Manuela Medina, "La Capitana," recruited singlehandedly an entire troop to fight in the battles for the independence of Mexico. Another woman, doña María Fermina Rivera, died for the cause, fighting side by side with the leader, Vicente Guerrero, in Chichihualco in 1821. Dolores Gertrudis Bocanegra de Lazo de la Vega, also known for her courage, lost her entire family in the fight for independence and was herself executed for her activities in the Plaza de Pátzcuaro on the first of October, 1817.

But it was in the revolutionary era from 1900 to 1917 that mestizo women found the amplest field for activism and militancy — as financiers, social workers, journalists, and in the armed services. Some great figures from this period are Carmen Serdán, Aquiles Serdán's sister, and his wife, doña Filomena del Valle de Serdán. They helped organize the first revolutionary forces in Puebla and gathered munitions for the men.

Although women had sacrificed fortunes, families, and lives during the revolution, their social and political status remained unchanged when the 1917 constitution was drawn up and adopted. Women began then to work for the civil rights they had helped win for others. Other great concerns for them also were the obliteration of poverty, the equitable distribution of land, and the improvement of life for women and children in Mexico.

Although the history of the Chicana is not as fully documented, we know that brave women in the United States also helped during the Mexican revolutionary period. María González of San Antonio helped political refugees financially, and Rosa R. de Carrigan and Rosa P. de Cornejo were active with the Partido Liberal in San Diego, California. We know that we have our martyrs and victims

1 *corregidora* a (woman) magistrate who has power to administer and enforce the law

of social injustice, such as "Juanita" of Downieville, California, who was lynched in 1851. And Chipita Rodríguez, who was sacrificed to gringo hatred in Texas, the only woman to be executed in the state. We know of many women who were victimized and martyred during the gringo pacification of the borderlands in the early part of this century. Francisco Becerra's aunt in Mercedes, Texas, was executed by the Rangers during one of their raids.

Our own Movement history has many illustrious women who are already part of history, and many more to be discovered as we record our accomplishments. Already a legend, María Hernández of Lytle, Texas, is a prominent Chicana educational and social reformer and orator in the San Antonio area. She has been active since the 1930s and is still going in 1973. And Virginia Músquiz of Crystal City, Texas, has been active politically since the 1950s and is, in the eyes of men and women of the Raza Unida, a vital copartner with Angel Gutiérrez in giving life to the party. Virginia Músquiz is a human dynamo of intelligence, dedication, diligence, and oratory skill, all in tremendous combination: she is indeed a superb model for all womanhood. She is a woman whom all Chicanas will strive to emulate in the future.

The Chicano community has traditionally encouraged the participation of aggressive women because of its more humanistic legal and educational tradition. And in the Movement in the United States also, the Chicana has enjoyed full participation in all aspects, whether social, political, or militant. So it is on the level of participation and on the numbers of women involved where Chicanas would like to improve.

We would like to see more women involved, and for their development not to be left to chance or to be on a selective basis; but for all women to have equal opportunity regardless of looks, availability, marital status, economic condition, or lack of aggressive tendencies. It would be ideal to have a great number of women, as visible and developed, as we now have male leaders within the Movement, both at the community and at the university levels. Chicanas with Chicana points of view should be encouraged to communicate to the Movement and to bring our needs and feelings as mothers, wives, sisters, college girls, and Movement women into focus for our brothers.

When women speak, the community listens. But they seldom speak. Women should have the freedom to help others develop. The greater numbers we have, the better. Let women develop with "Chicano conscience," with nurturance and guidance from developed activists, and with the knowledge of the glorious Chicana martyrs and heroines.

When Chicanas can view the past and see their femininity and feminism in this context, they will recognize past and present Movement models, and we can face any feminist movement and still remain firmly within our Raza. We can be intelligently aware of the motives of the white woman's liberation movement and react intelligently to their rhetoric and recruitment efforts. We can, if we so desire, use our political arm, the Raza Unida party, to wrestle power and lobby on an equal basis, visibly and independently, in the nation, in political groups such as the National Women's Political Caucus.

There has always been feminism in our ranks and there will continue to be as long as Chicanas live and breathe in the Movement, but we must see to it that we specify philosophical direction and that our feminist expression will be our own and coherent with our Raza's goals in cultural areas which are ours. Chicanas will direct their own destiny.

Edmund Villaseñor

The Sánchez Sisters

This excerpt from Macho! *presents the encounter of three strong and distinct personalities: Gloria Sánchez, Lydia Sánchez, and Roberto García, whom the reader met earlier (page 12) in his native Mexican village. Roberto has entered the United States illegally by this time and is working precariously. In this novel of the 1960s Edmund Villaseñor has sought to illustrate and to highlight his characters' differing attitudes about the roles of men and women.*

The older daughter was eighteen, three months younger than Roberto, and she wore a dress and her name was Gloria Sánchez and her family came from Chihuahua. Her father had been an immigrated green carder,[1] then five years later had become an American citizen and brought his family over from Mexico. His two daughters had been born here in California. He no longer followed the harvest from Yuma to Sacramento to Salinas. He lived here, near Acampo, permanently so he could send his children to school. Gloria, the most educated of the family, had finished high school and last year had got a scholarship to attend a junior college. She had always loved to read books, go to school, and study history and geography, and in high school her Spanish teacher had come and talked to her parents and told them he would try to get her a scholarship. She was a good student, and in the last few years, because of Chávez and Kennedy and many others, Mexican Americans now had much opportunity to get scholarships. So Gloria's Spanish teacher finally got her a scholarship and now she only worked at picking fruit in the summers

1 *green carder* holder of an entry permit that gives one the official status of a resident alien

so she could buy her school clothes and not be too much a burden on her parents.

After dinner she and Roberto talked at the table while her mother sat there with them. The men had gone outside. Roberto had stayed behind on the pretense that he was still hungry. He now sat there, playing with his food, trying to eat another bite, but unable. The mother smiled. She guessed his situation but wouldn't leave. She stayed there, sitting next to her elder daughter. Her daughter was telling Roberto about her scholarship and how the great benevolent César Chávez had helped her and all Chicanos. Roberto said nothing.

Gloria asked him what he thought of the great César Chávez.

He shook his head and said he didn't know . . . "Nada, nada." [2] All he knew was what he had seen at a certain huelga.[3] She became interested, and he told her the story of that strike as he had seen it.

"And you didn't walk across those picket lines and help! Eh?" She was terribly excited. "What kind of Mexican are you? A coward!"

"Gloria!" snapped her mother. "Hold your tongue! You have no right to raise your voice at this young man."

But Gloria would not be quieted. She continued accusing, demanding, and yelling. Roberto was red in the face. He finally stood up. Fast! Gloria's eyes went large. There he stood . . . heavy. Boss. Good. And the bird of fear flew through her, and she was afraid, and yet . . . the woman in her held in admiration of the powerful look of this young man.

"Thank you for dinner, señora," said Roberto to her mother. He was speaking very formally, and he was not addressing her, the daughter. "I have not known such wonderful cooking since I left home. . . ." He stepped back away. He picked up his straw hat. "And I thank you," he said to Gloria in a less formal tone of voice. The younger

2 *nada* nothing
3 *huelga* strike

sister was over there doing the dishes. "Both of you, thank you."

And he began to leave, when the younger girl, who was seventeen and a senior in high school and not such a good student, said, "Please, tell me one thing before you go." Roberto stopped. She brushed back her hair with the back of her hand. Her hand was covered with white wet suds. "Tell me, did you make more money or less money when Chávez came?"

He blinked his eyes. He had not noticed this girl all evening. She was still in boots and pants and long-sleeved shirt. She looked more like a boy than a girl. She was tall for a Mexican girl. She was five foot six and could pick fruit faster than most men. She had quick hands and quick feet, and at school she was on the track team, and she loved sports and outside work. Books bored her. She was not a good student.

"I lost money," said Roberto.

This young sister, Lydia, smiled, nodded, and went back to doing the dishes. "I thought so," she said. "Chávez isn't so good. A real worker does not need him."

"No!" yelled Gloria. "You are wrong! You and my ignorant brothers don't understand. We are being discriminated against and. . . ." She turned to Roberto. "Did you make good money all year long?"

"Yes," said Roberto. "I worked hard and made much money."

"How much? Do you have any idea what the national average is? Eh? Of course you don't, and this winter you will starve! You will not be able — "

Roberto bowed courteously. "With your permission, señora," he said to the mother, "I'm going outside with the men. Thank you."

And he went out without addressing the girls, and he heard Lydia, the younger sister, burst out laughing and tell Gloria that she was one very dumb woman. She knew so much from books and yet a good-looking boy turns her on and she insults him and sends him running. Gloria yelled at her. Lydia laughed. The mother spoke loudly.

All went quiet.

Roberto breathed . . . and went out to see the men. They were under a tree by the tall wire fence. They were smoking and passing around a small bottle. He sat down on the good earth. The earth was warm to his Levi's. The heat of the day lingered long into the night. He sipped from the bottle. It was whiskey. He made a face and gave a sound of relief as it traveled down his throat. He exhaled and listened to their conversation. They were talking about Chávez and his union.

RAYMOND BARRIO

Mi Vida

In 1969, when Raymond Barrio was unable to interest any major publishing company in his novel, he set up a printing press in his garage and began printing and distributing The Plum Plum Pickers *himself. Now published by a major company, Barrio's story of migrant farmworkers in California is reaching a wide readership. Instead of trying to develop the epic experiences of great numbers of people in his novel, Barrio has chosen to focus on the day-to-day drama of particular individuals like Lupe Gutiérrez, who appears in this excerpt. The experiences that she refers to in "Mi Vida" ("My Life") are not at all unusual; rather, they typify the situation of thousands of migrant families who share an entire way of life.*

"Plenty good fat corn, mi vida, my life!" Manuel planted a big kiss on Lupe's attractive neck, then guzzled down the other half of his glass of red vino. "I shall make you a necklace of beautiful green esmeraldas, greener than your eyes. You watch, you witch, my chula,[1] my precious wife, you wait and see!"

Lupe brushed him off, smiling, happy to see him happy. "How many times must I tell you my eyes are not green."

"Beautiful, beautiful — "

It was nice to hear his compliments. The dust, the never-ending dust from the outside, the dirt and earth and grease and grime covering the torn linoleum floor with its gritty film exasperated Lupe more than anything else about the shack.

"Get away," she said, pushing him with her elbow as she swung the wet mop around.

1 *chula* beautiful

"Eh, mujer,"[2] he said, stepping back cautiously. "You are in a bad mood, I see."

"No, I am not," she said, looking up, becoming genuinely annoyed that he could be so dense. "It is you."

"But you are the one who just struck me."

"I did not."

"You jabbed me with your elbow, mi corazón,"[3] he said as politely as possible, trying to show how wrong she was.

"You are the one who is wrong. You were standing in the way, and I must do my work, and you ran into me."

"I suppose you think that I do not work."

Though it was late in the day, the heat was still punishing them through the open unscreened door. The heat of anger, born of exasperation, escalating on frustration, pushing through the coolest part of her composure, tempted her temper.

"I suppose," he repeated deliberately, "that you do not think I work."

So. He was looking for a fight. Well, she was ready. He would find out. Her nerves tightened as he walked over to the crib and fondled the sleeping baby's head.

"You will wake Cati up," she said, trying to control her rising anger.

"So?" The infant, startled, moved and wiggled her legs, scowling and wrinkling her tiny features. Then she let out a short, sharp, strident yelp, her eyes still shut tight.

"There, I told you. Couldn't you leave her alone?"

"But I did not wake her. I only — "

"Yes, I, always I. You never realize that it is I who must fight her when she's awake, and feed her, and change her."

Frowning, Manuel lifted the screaming infant in his strong, rough, calloused hands. He pressed the child's face to his shoulder. The baby's shrieks gradually subsided. "¿Qué pasó, gordita?"[4] he murmured, holding her coconut head to his face, smelling her. "That baby smell is good. That baby sweat, I like it." He walked over to the kitchen

2 *mujer* woman
3 *mi corazón* my sweetheart
4 *"¿Qué pasó, gordita?"* "What happened, my cute chubby one?"

table, picking up a diaper and the can of talcum powder along the way, and swiftly removed the baby's soaked and pungent diaper. He dusted her bottom with the talc, then pinned the clean diaper on. "There," he said quietly. "Now you have a nice dry diaper on."

Lupe slammed the mop to the floor. "SO! You think you are the one big help, do you? What do you do about the dishes, big man? And the floor? And the dozens and dozens of times I change her diapers when you aren't around? And tonight's dinner? Why don't you take me out to dinner? You're ashamed to, isn't that it? You're ashamed of my clothes. Does it not ever bother you that I haven't one single decent thing to wear?"

"Enough, mujer."

"Why? Why is that enough? Are you pleased with yourself?" Crushed between misery and frustration, Lupe felt a sudden release from her anger. What was the matter with him? Couldn't he, couldn't he, see how she, she, she was suffering? Complaints? What complaints? What was she complaining about? How long was she going to have to put up with these stupid pressures! "All this running around, running from house to shack, from town to village, from farm to farm, never having the rent, or change for the laundry machines." She barely stopped for breath. "I've had enough, you hear. Enough. You think you can drag us from place to place and give us a few frijoles — "

"Enough, mujer," said Manuel in a low voice.

"Sí — frijoles. This is what you call the good life, eh. And even boast of it. In Mexico — and nobody can tell — "

"Woman, mujer, I said enough, basta."

"What? What enough? Go on. What are you going to say? Are you going to try for a better job? Is that it, or what?"

He looked at her. He put the baby slowly back in her crib. Cati started screaming again. He put his hat on and turned to the door.

"Sure. Of course. Go on. You big man. Go on out and enjoy yourself. Drink. Andale, borracho.[5] Run. Run away. That's the way. Go on, you coward. And when you get

5 *Andale, borracho.* Go on, you drunk.

back you can be sure of one thing: You can be sure that I won't be here nor will any of the children."

He left. He closed the door quietly behind him.

Her fury mounted. She knew what he would do. He would go to the Golden Cork and in broad daylight get a good drunk on. That was his historic way. He would stay drunk for a day and a night. And he would be no good for work for another day. And he would put in danger all the confidence he'd spent these weeks and months building up. He would say he was sick. "Just another drunken Mexican" was what his bosses would say, and so would that evil contratista,[6] Roberto Morales.

She snapped. She just didn't care any more. Anger shattered her usual self-control and paralyzed her good sense. She slammed clothing into the old cardboard suitcase that had been standing in the corner. Manuelito's pants, underclothes, and Mariquita's dresses, and the baby's diapers.

"Where we going, Mama?" The two youngsters, in from the shade-speckled out-of-doors, danced around her feet.

"I don't know, I don't know," she cried, pushing them away from her. "Somewhere."

They backed off, respecting her great anger. Holding the baby in one arm, the box in the other, she held the screen door open for the children to scamper through. As she turned to release the door, she felt herself grasped firmly around the waist and lifted clear into the air. The box was snatched from her hand.

"You put me down!!" she screamed, kicking.

"Not until you promise to behave," said Manuel. He carried her and the baby bodily back into the shack and set her down. "Why must you do this to me, my heart?"

"Why? Why?" she screamed back. "Because I am going out of my mind. That is why. What did you think?"

"But I do not see why, corazón," he said softly.

And then in a flash she saw that he really did not see. She buried her face in Cati's blanket, crying with her.

Outwardly, physically, Manuel was rough and strong.

6 *contratista* labor contractor

Inside he was soft and kind and even innocent. He really did not see the many hurts and the many complications that constantly chipped away her reserve, her resolve, her plans, her peace of mind, her dreams. One moment angry, in the next instant she crumpled in a heap to the floor, bending over the baby moaning, sobbing, rocking back and forth. "Why why why? God, God, God." Sobbing over and over. "Por qué por qué por qué? Dios, dios, dios."

"Mi corazón," said Manuel tenderly, sitting beside her on the floor. Lifting the crying baby gently away from her. "You must stop. Come. Don't cry any more."

Little by little she composed herself. He kept murmuring to her, embracing her, and soon her sobs subsided. "I'm all right," she said after a while.

"You are quite upset, my heart, why? What is it that is twisting you all up?"

He truly did not know. "Nothing. No, no. Nothing."

"Then listen to me, Lupe. I have a big idea. Let us go down to a restaurant tonight for our dinner."

"No, no, Manuel. You know we cannot afford it."

"But you need some diversion, some distraction."

"That is why you offer it?" she said, a little sharply. Suddenly she was afraid her anger would return; he felt it too.

"No, corazón, no. Well, yes, maybe, in a way. And why not? I have earned a good packet today."

Yes, he'd made good money that day. But what about tomorrow? More important — what about November? And December? She held her tongue. She was tempted by the restaurant, she loved having a meal served to her at a table, but her practical nature won out. "No. I'm much better now, Manuel."

She stood up. He stood up beside her, solicitous, watching her, and with a great surge of warmth she realized she'd pushed too far. Embracing him, she said, "You bruto, you can go to the store for the tortillas if you want to. Do you want to? I'll make tacos."

Ay, tacos! His favorite dish. Because of the hard work it took, all that frying and spluttering hot hot fat, he knew she was in control of herself again. He would get her a little pot of geraniums.

La Vida

Life

then the day-done sun glistened, burned deeply,
disappearing into my eyes blinking: innocently
i blinked toward the towering twilight.

Tino Villanueva

LEROY QUINTANA

piñones

In these lines a poet suggests a conclusion about life by contrasting details from past days with those of the present. The piñones he mentions are the piñon (pine) nuts traditionally associated with New Mexico. After sharing Leroy Quintana's "remembrance of things past," readers may be stimulated to recall and to re-create details from their own childhood days. Quintana is on the faculty at New Mexico State University.

when i was young
we would sit by
an old firewood stove
watching my grandmother make candy,
listening to the stories
my grandparents would tell
about "the old days"
                                        and eat piñones

now we belong
to a supersonic age
and have college degrees.
we sit around color t.v. sets
watching the super bowl
listening to howard cosell,
stories of rioting, war, inflation
                              and eat piñones

SABINE ULIBARRÍ

The Stuffing of the Lord

Much of the heritage and many of the traditions from Spain have been maintained by the people of New Mexico since the first Spanish settlers entered the area in 1598. Tierra Amarilla ("Yellow Land") is the name of the small town in northern New Mexico where Sabine Ulibarrí was born and still lives. He used the name of the town as the title of his first collection of short stories. Like most of the stories from Tierra Amarilla, *"The Stuffing of the Lord" (which appears here in a translation from the original Spanish) is notable for the author's lively style and his nostalgic recreation of an entire society. Dr. Ulibarrí is a professor at the University of New Mexico.*

Father Benito almost saved my soul. Certainly he put me on the road to salvation, a feat which shocked and surprised my parents and elicited admiring exclamations from all the townsfolk. And wherever he may now be, Father Benito probably still regards me as saved.

The truth is that up to the age of twelve I had never shown the least interest in religion, much less any inclination to the priesthood or any other hood, priestly or otherwise. I had, in fact, given many indications of traveling in the opposite direction.

That is the way things were going when Father Benito came to Tierra Amarilla for the first time. Tierra Amarilla has never been the same since that day, nor have any of us who used to live there. The good father brought us light and life, tenderness and joy. He filled the town with talk and gaiety. He drew us to the Kingdom of Heaven by the strangest method ever used in the history of religion. If dying of laughter is a good thing, Father Benito brought us to a good death many, many times.

He had a round, bald head like a pale pumpkin. In the

center of the tremendous hood of the Franciscan habit, it seemed to be loose, placed there without reason. Its position looked so precarious that one expected to see it roll from its place at any moment. On his saintly, round, slightly foolish face there was always a fixed smile — a truly beatific expression. He wore rimless glasses, out of style even then, on the end of his nose. I don't know why. Certainly it was not for seeing. Perhaps they were the transparent vestments for an extremely naked face. It was a nudity, stemming from innocence, turned virtue and purity. His small paunch, round as the loaves of San Roque,[1] was supported by a white cord. Biblical sandals completed the angelic image of the priest who filled the entire valley of Tierra Amarilla with affection and harmony.

He was like the sun. When he passed along the street, he scattered smiles and good humor about him, banishing shadows, warming the dying, animating the conversation, provoking an occasional burst of laughter. Mirth was his constant companion.

He spoke terrible Spanish, fluent but mutilated. He could not pronounce the word reino in his favorite expression, el reino de Dios (the Kingdom of God), but he repeated it so often that it acquired a strange, fatal importance. Saying mass, he used to chant in magisterial tones, "In order to enter into the relleno of God. . . ." Relleno, dear readers, sounds a little like reino, but it means "stuffing"! While the words and the ascending intonation seemed to build a stairway to heavenly places, the faithful were in misery. They were broken up. They squirmed, they hunched their shoulders and lowered their heads. Spasms. Contortions. Agony. Fierce and fatal laughter, unbearable because it had to be contained.

The Father's ignorance of the language forced him to inquire about words when he was preparing his sermons. On one occasion, he asked a waggish character the word for "foundation," since he planned to preach a sermon about the poor condition of the substructure of the church.

1 *San Roque* saint who, when stricken with the plague, was brought bread each day by a faithful hound

Nobody ever stayed away from mass while Father Benito was in Tierra Amarilla. As usual, the church was full. The good priest began to scold us with his usual sincerity and fervor.

"You neglect your church. You are a disgrace to your religion. Today there will be a special collection to provide fundaments for this church. The fundaments we have now are filthy, they have a bad odor. . . ." Nobody heard another word.

I doubt that in the history of Catholicism any priest ever had as unusual and eccentric an audience as Father Benito — without his ever knowing it. It was a congregation of convulsed faces, puffed cheeks, trembling chins, and bulging eyes. Noses were blown. Arms and legs twitched. Ears turned purple. Groans, moans, stifled cries — strange noises. The parishioners lowered their heads, bit their lips, held their stomachs, shuddered and shook. They were in agony.

The saintly priest from his pulpit, blind and deaf to what was going on, looked over his glasses at the bowed heads of the faithful. He saw them overcome by religious fervor. Virtuous and sincere, he gave us his best, he became more and more eloquent, he soared to the heights of passionate feeling.

All of us left the church exhausted. Pale, spent, with tears still in our eyes. We went home in silence. Without speaking. Without laughing. Without strength for anything else. Later, some other day, we would laugh. Then we would talk it over. Not now. Suppressed laughter is a savage beast in a cage.

Of course, nobody talked about anything else. The acolytes[2] talked, too. They said that our beloved priest had one other peculiarity that they alone knew about. He did not like wine! The nuns always filled the little jar for communion, and he left it almost full. I had heard my father and other men say that priests had the best wine in the world. For that reason and no other, I entered on the path of salvation.

For the first time I began to pay attention at cate-

2 *acolytes* altar boys, who assist the priest at mass

chism. I stopped asking the impertinent questions that had brought me so many catholic, apostolic, and Roman[3] lumps on the head. I learned to lower my eyes properly and humbly at the least pretext and also to roll them piously upward toward the electric light bulb among the cracks and spider webs of the ceiling. I answered the questions of the priests and the nuns correctly, without creating the least disturbance. In short, I became so extremely sanctimonious that I surpassed the oldest and ugliest female fanatics of the area.

My parents did not know about all this, since it happened at school. Occasionally an aunt or a friend would remark to my mother that I was behaving myself very well and that it was high time. Once, when this happened in my presence, my mother looked at me suspiciously. The conversation continued, however, and she forgot about it. I never knew whether my father found out.

But in the convent school the word certainly got around. The happiness of the sisters was almost more than they could bear. It was a miracle. I had been a student of theirs for six years, and those six years had been purgatory for them — and for me, too. For a long time I carried a body full of welts as holy testimony to my suffering.

No one can possibly know the joy — I mean delirium — I should say ecstasy — of a devoted sister who carries an unregenerate, submissive sinner and lays him in the lap of the Lord. I saw their rhapsodic glances and trembled, but not with pleasure. There is something frenzied and frightening about a woman in ecstasy. When I saw them, my hair stood on end, or as one could say, reached toward heaven. The latter seemed to be their interpretation.

They became gentle, sweet, and kindly toward me. In my new role of lamb, or little suckling pig, I accepted their kindnesses. The most generous of all was Sister Generosa.

The nuns had charge of the altar and of dressing the saints. One day, when I felt that my campaign had achieved its purpose, I presented myself to be dressed — as an altar

3 *catholic, apostolic, and Roman* probably a humorous reference to a phrase in the creed that members of the catechism class would have learned

boy, of course. That day there was rejoicing in the fields of the Lord, at least in one of them.

Thus began my religious career. It soon became evident that there was great promise in the new acolyte. During the Mea Culpa[4] my chest-pounding resounded throughout the tiny temple. My amens were the most amenable that had ever been heard in that region. All the way to the Ite Missa Est[5] I was the most attentive and zealous of the crowd.

There were two altar boys. Completely organized. The priest fawned upon by the good ladies of the town. The sisters lining up the children. We tidying up, folding, arranging, in the sacristy.[6] One swallow for me. One for you. Another for me. First we drank the wine and then we sniffed the jar dry. When Sister Generosa came in, the heavenly jar was empty, completely clean. Neither she nor any of the sisters ever knew that Father Benito did not like wine.

I accompanied Father Benito to many a wedding and many a funeral. He with his hyssop and I with the censer.[7] The odor of sanctity must be something like the smell of that smoke. At all these festivities they served the priest first from the best they had, then his assistant, naturally. For the intelligent assistant there is a good swig behind each blessing and a blessing in each swig. I always returned from these expeditions spiritually enriched. That life was becoming more and more fascinating to me.

My mother always accompanied me to high mass, the one read by Father Benito. I was now beginning to give her something to be proud of, whereas formerly I had given her only trouble. At least that is what I thought, although I frequently suspected that she was not really convinced of my conversion. But at any rate, the women of the town who used to have so many complaints about me now heaped me

4 *Mea Culpa* part of the Latin mass in which there was a confession of fault. The words mean "through my fault."

5 *Ite Missa Est* "Go; the mass is ended."

6 *sacristy* room in a church building where clerical robes, altar linen, etc., are kept

7 *hyssop, censer* references to sprinkling with holy water and using incense

with praises. It was a well-deserved rest for my mother.

My father never saw me or heard me at the altar, except for my baptism and first communion. Due to a series of unexpected incidents he had to go on trips most weekends when I was displaying my chest-beating and my amenable amens. Some Sundays he had to go to six o'clock mass because of pressing duties. And unfortunately he contracted a mysterious illness which struck him on five successive Sundays and prevented his attending mass. His friends were much concerned, for they said he had not been seen for months. This troubled me a great deal. How I wanted to impress him — for the first time! Wasn't I now a real personality?

The usual thing happened to us. They took our good Father Benito away from us. I did not know what to do. My whole new life was abruptly ended. We said good-bye. I, with deeply sincere tears. He, with a sad smile. There are priests who inspire heartfelt love, others who are loved from a sense of duty, and — one must confess — some who are never loved at all. Father Benito belonged to the first group.

The day he left, the whole town came out to bid him good-bye. I do not think there was a dry eye in the crowd. That innocent spirit went away without knowing what he had brought us, without knowing what had happened. Without knowing what he was taking away with him. He carried with him much of the day's brightness, much laughter, and much happiness. He left us only the knowledge that we would never again know the same measure of those qualities. I believe that I felt his departure more than anyone else.

I returned to my post the next Sunday with the new priest. It was not the same. My chest-pounding sounded dull and hollow. My amens lacked the old resonance. When the moment of communion arrived, I poured the accustomed amount of the saramental wine. The priest shook the divine vessel impatiently. Reluctantly I poured a little more. He insisted. Finally I poured it all.

How indecent that seemed to me! What bad taste! I was — well, not raging, because that would have been a sacrilege at the altar — but something very much like it until the Ite Missa Est, which rang down the final curtain on my religious career.

I returned to my old ways and my old pranks. I acted almost as I had before — almost but not quite. Something new, something unforeseen, had come to me in Father Benito's wine. I could not forget the good priest. My parents were surprised once more, but I think they were relieved and secretly thanked God. One thing is sure: my father no longer had to go away on Sundays, and his mysterious illness disappeared. Once again we went to mass as a family. My mother between us giving a pinch to my father and another to me in moments when they were needed.

The years passed. My parents had died by this time. My siblings and I were now living in Santa Fe. We saw in the newspaper that a friend of ours, Flavio Hernández, had died. The rosary would be in the Salazar Funeral Home, and Father Benito would conduct the service!

I don't know which of our two motives was more powerful. We wanted to pay our respects to the dead, but we were also very eager to see Father Benito again. When we reached the mortuary, which was unfamiliar to us, we followed some people who were entering and found ourselves in a chapel where the deceased lay.

My sister, my brother, and I entered respectfully, our heads bowed. We threaded our way through the crowd, approached the coffin, knelt, and began to pray. I tried to think about my prayers, but my thoughts kept going back to Tierra Amarilla and Father Benito. I remembered that at that time I had a very vague idea of what the Kingdom of God might be, but that I had a very clear and grotesque image of what the relleno de Dios might be. The revival of that memory started in me the silent tickling of a mad mirth. There is no laughter so wicked as that which strikes in a serious or sacred place.

I was trying to control myself when my brother nudged me. I heard a frightened whisper, "That isn't Flavio!" I raise my eyes and look. Not only is it not Flavio, but is a woman! I nudge my sister. She looks. We all stare. We turn our heads. We are surrounded by people we don't know.

Suddenly, without any warning, wild laughter swirls inside us. The absurdity of that situation is too much. We do everything possible to control ourselves, but to no avail. We bite our lips. Our abdomens ache. Our faces become livid, congested. The suffering is indescribable. One of the others breaks out in a snort. We have to hide this, cover it up. I begin to weep noisily. My brother and sister follow my lead. Our tears flow freely. Our cries become more and more despairing. Hastily we stumble out, blind with tears and suffering. The real mourners have nothing to complain about. Our lamentations were certainly the hit of the year and the pride of the mortuary.

We reached home exhausted, literally sick. We should laugh and talk about it another day, but now it was impossible, as in the days of Father Benito and his masses. That night Father Benito made us laugh as he had in the old days. Without even seeing him. His physical presence was not needed. His trademark is laughter.

Always, when someone laughs deeply and helplessly, I think about the good father and laugh, too. And wonder how many souls may have reached heaven, having died laughing, saved that way by Saint Benito. I don't know what has become of him, but I am sure that he is still living. Certainly the day he enters the relleno de Dios, we will hear the peals of laughter, the cries, the guffaws, and the moans of the saints and the little angels — all this followed by long silences.

Fray Angélico Chávez

Rattlesnake

Since people first started sketching the outlines of animals on cave walls, artists and poets have tried to capture and re-create the essence of living things. With great economy of words, yet adhering to a conventional pattern of rhyme and rhythm, Fray ("Friar") Chávez here has created a series of remarkable images. A retired member of the Franciscan order, Fray Chávez lives in his native New Mexico. He has published several collections of poetry.

Line of beauty scrawled alive
by God's finger on the sand,
diamond-patterned inlaid band
scrolling inward like a hive —

Stay away,
crawl-created,
articulated
coil of cloisonné!

FLOYD SALAS

Dead Time

Published in 1967, Tattoo the Wicked Cross *tells about the experiences of young Aaron D'Aragon in reform school. The title of this powerful novel refers to the cross with projecting rays above that pachucos, or gang youths (page 61), used as their identifying sign. The title of this excerpt from the first chapter refers to an inmate's first days in such an institution, before he is assigned to a dormitory or a work detail. Born in Colorado, Floyd Salas himself served time in several California institutions before pursuing a literary career. Since those troubled days, however, Salas has gone on to win several scholarships as well as literary awards and distinctions.*

The gilt metal letters above the main gate, THE GOLDEN GATE INSTITUTE OF INDUSTRY & REFORM, were dull in the overcast spring morning, but they remained vivid in Aaron's mind as he stepped on short wobbly legs into the institute office.

A pungent odor of Pinesol disinfectant, laced with the smells of stale wax and worn metal furniture, had the familiar reek of the airless detention-home halls he had left only two hours before; they gave him the feeling that he had dreamed of or had been in this very office before, and they reminded him that his brother John had told him to remember . . . something, but he could not recall what it was.

The long bench which stretched away from him the length of the gray wall was familiar, too, and so were the fluorescent tubes of light burning like ribs of hot ice on the low ceiling and frosting the thick coat of varnish on the high counter which divided the room.

The big man in khaki who sat typing on the opposite side of the counter could have been any man in the detention home, and his command to sit down could have come from any of their indistinguishable mouths.

Aaron sat quickly down. He sat erect, with his hands clasped in the lap of the old Boy Scout pants he had worn for the trip, his old gym shoes just touching the floor, his faded sweatshirt not touching the wall. The probation officer entered the office carrying a large manila envelope.

But the dull metal letters of the sign still stood like bars before him and between him and what he was supposed to remember. They had stood like giant bars across his last glimpse of the northern California highway as the gate closed behind him. They had barred the windshield of the black state car and the blank side of the official pass that the guard had put under the wiper before the car began its slow, creeping drive up the paved road, which circled like a noose through the main grounds.

They had stood like fence posts across the open fields inside the barbed-wire institute fence. They had been as tall and solemn as the ash-brown twin rows of eucalyptus trees which stood guard on opposite sides of the entrance drive. They had striped the flat white institute buildings. They had stood as stiff and important as the flagpole in front of the office, and had spaced the sloping lawn of the hillside there with the significance of statues on graveyard plots.

The metal letters now masked the face of the close-cropped gray head, with the shaved sideburns, which was decapitated by the counter, and also replaced the metal clock hands on the wall. They sat on the floor as heavily as the steel cabinets, in which the manila envelope with his life history would be filed. They let less daylight through the windows than the Venetian blinds. The typewriter spelled them out with its distracting clack-clack instead of what he was supposed to remember, although he kept telling himself that a thousand other guys had already been through the gate.

"C'mere," the man ordered.

And Aaron forgot the letters, for the khaki bulk of the man seemed to swell with each step he took toward the counter until he was directly beneath the mountainous chest and shoulders.

"My name is Mr. Toothman," the man said and took the manila envelope from the probation officer in return for a disinterested shake of his fingers.

"My job is to make sure you do your time here without making a nuisance of yourself. And your job is to make sure you obey all the rules, all day, every day, and you'll do your time without getting yourself hurt. Got me?" the man asked and glared at Aaron from short-lidded, dry and unblinking eyes.

"Yes . . ." Aaron said, in a thin voice.

"What?" the man asked and poked down with his blunt nose.

"Yes!" Aaron blurted out, his tongue darting out and over his full lips in a nervous action.

There was a short, welcome pause in which the man took a manila folder out of the manila envelope, flipped its cover open, and studied Aaron's record, a pause in which Aaron tried to remember again, a pause briefly interrupted by the slight monotone of the probation officer:

"He behaved himself on the way up here. Seems scared and ready to learn his lesson, and they told me he buckled down pretty quick at the detention home."

The lipless gap that served for the man's mouth opened slightly, then closed, as if taking an impatient and barely tolerant breath. The probation officer leaned on the counter with an indifferent slouch, propping his elbow on it, his soiled gray suit falling in sacklike folds to his scuffed shoes, his colorless eyes neither looking at nor avoiding the man's stare, looking nowhere, looking at nothing; but the colorless lips flickered in a smile when the man started reading again.

The smile and the timbreless voice surprised Aaron, for the probation officer had hardly spoken during the hundred-mile trip, and now to hear him speak in his defense was totally unexpected. For the first time he saw the mild neutrality in the probation officer's face, saw a complexion neither pale nor tanned, eyes of no distinguishable color, not even a purposeful gray, but without contempt nor any desire to punish in them.

"Aaron D'Aragon . . ." the man said, commenting aloud on Aaron's crime-jacket. "Never been arrested for theft but with five arrests for fighting, and all within two years, and in each case involving a gang which was led by him. You're Big Shot Instigator, huh?"

"I . . . I . . . yes," Aaron said, submitting as he knew he had to, as he had during the long two months in the detention home; but he was ashamed of his stutter, and he felt a blush stain his cheeks.

"It's hard to believe such a little squirt could lead a gang of mostly older boys, a couple of them with records, too. You're not even five feet tall and you're fifteen, aren't chou?" the man asked, then demanded, without waiting for an answer: "Answer! It says here, you've always got an answer for everything. Answer!"

"Yes," Aaron replied, making sure he said it clearly; and the ease with which he answered under the man's pressure gave him courage, so that he stood straighter, squared his narrow shoulders, brought his legs together, and lifted his chin slightly but carefully so as not to appear defiant, not to show the slightest hint of cockiness.

Occasionally the man looked up from the folder and stared dry-eyed and unblinking at Aaron, as if for verification; and Aaron found that he could endure the stare without a shirking sideward glance, could look past the carefully curled black lock of his hair and prove that he had nothing to hide, that he was ready to do his time, do it good, get it over with, get back out on the streets, and start living again.

The man slapped the folder closed and dropped it on a desk, lifted the counter leaf, forcing the probation officer to jerk back to keep his arm from being slammed against the wall, and muttered something as he stepped past him. The colorless fingers of the probation officer snapped on the brim of the gray hat in a silent good-bye, and the screen door squeaked open and clapped shut.

To catch up with the man Aaron had to skip across the room, hurry out the back door, cross a gravel clearing, his footsteps sharp as a watchdog's bark in his ears, and run up the concrete steps of another building. Here he realized he was passing through the hospital corridor, odorous with antiseptics, and was aware of a nurse's stiff white cap, the rustle of her starched uniform, and her mumbled greeting to the man. The next flight of stairs required an extra effort, for his knees were weakening and his legs were growing heavy, and he was afraid he would stumble as he walked down a dark corridor lined with wooden cell doors to a shower room at its far end.

"Get those clothes off," the man said; and Aaron scratched his chest and tore a button from his trouser fly in his nervous haste to undress quickly under the man's impatient stare. "Okay, now get in that shower and make it quick, and get that stinking grease out of your hair."

Aaron stepped into the punishing sting of hot water, letting it tattoo his head, briefly rubbed soap into his scalp, turned the cold water on, and let it numb his flesh and every concern except getting out of it. Then he hurried to rub down with the towel and slip on a woolen nightgown before the man got angry, and he found himself trying to remember once again and to listen to the man, too, as he was being locked in a cell.

"You'll stay here until the doctor's examined you, until that haircut has been clipped, and a job's been found for you. If you behave, you'll be treated square and you'll do less time. But if you act up and play the wise punk, I'll teach you something. I'll make you act like a man while you're here or break you in trying. And if you get too tough for the institute, you'll get committed to Youth Authority, and maybe those boys in the state reform schools will teach you what tough is? Got me?" the man asked in a tone as brittle as the shine of his eyes.

"Got me, I said?"

"Huh?" Aaron said, but the command sharpened his memory.

"Got me?"

"Oh, yes. Yes," Aaron said.

"Yes! Yes! Yes!" he kept repeating to the thick gray door which shut in his face.

He cocked his left hand to slam it against the door.

But a long, quavering breath escaped from him, and he dropped his clenched hands to his sides, rubbed his sweating palms against the thick nap of the nightgown, made an about-face, and the soles of his feet squeaked with friction.

He gazed absentmindedly about the cell until he noticed a gray brushstroke on the hardwood floor, where a careless painter had run off the baseboard. He fixed his eyes hypnotically upon it for some time. The stroke would blur occasionally, come into focus, and blur again.

He shook his head to clear it and, looking for more defects, let his sight follow the baseboard to the back corner of the cell, let it turn there and follow the board along the back wall into the film of dust and darkness under the radiator, let it glide up to the top of the radiator's accordion ridges, when he noticed odd traces of shadow on the wall above that suggested letters.

He squinted his eyes and tried to decipher them without moving from his position, but he was unable to, and he began to take slow steps toward them, trying to discover at what distance he could.

By the third lagging step, he felt his pulse quicken, for he could distinguish a cross with three rays above it; and another step brought the numbers 1 and, possibly, a 5 of a date into view; and with another step, he guessed that a circled indentation was in reality a twisted heart, with a pachuco cross planted into the cleft between the lobes and the year 1945 scratched below the tip. But the faint hollows within the clumsy heart remained obscure until he reached the wall and ran his finger slowly over the thick coat of gray paint.

He felt his sense of triumph grow into admiration as he traced the name RICKY DE LA CRUZ across both lobes of the heart, made out a plus mark, and spelled out the EVA that was wedged into the heart's point. For the guy must have spent days of stolen spoon-handle labor carving that five-inch heart into the bare institute wall, and he had to be full of guts and love to do it, because he knew he was going to have to suffer for it. Yet he had so much guts he carved it in the most conspicuous spot in the cell, where it could be seen by anyone and everybody who looked through the glass slot, and *so that* it would be seen by anyone and everyone.

Aaron wished he had a spoon, too, to prove *he* had the guts to love, to prove that neither the Man nor the cell nor dead time could kill either his guts or his love, to prove what the thick, useless paint and the year that had passed had proved for Ricky De La Cruz, to prove that he, like Ricky De La Cruz, was greater than the cell!

RAÚL R. SALINAS

sinfonía serrana

The title of this poem can be translated as "symphony to a woman from the mountains." When poets use their craft to communicate a thought or message to a specific person, their lines can also have significance for other readers, whose experience it may reflect or illuminate in some way. This is why, even though Raúl Salinas seems to address these lines to a real person, we can understand the thought and appreciate the feelings that they express. Salinas began to write while in prison: in another poem he explains that writing saved him "from insanity's hungry jaws." Today he teaches creative writing at a state university in the Northwest.

how can
i
sing you
songs of love

when all
i
ever learned were
howls of hate

i
cannot gift you
with
bouquets of joy

my
garden only yields
wild
weeds of sorrow

you
asked for the sun
i
could not provide

the
blame is not yours

i
wanted the moon
i
cried for the moon

when the
wrappings came off
i found
plastic and sham

so
to nurse both our
wounds from the
thorns of deceit

we
will sign our
last love-pact
in blood

with
the scalpel of loneliness
i'll carve you a sliver
of my soul

to
paste up in
the scrapbook
of your heart

even
tho'
i
know

poems
don't bring in
much money
these days

raúlrsalinas
leavenworth penitentiary
1971

José Antonio Villarreal

The World of Richard Rubio

José Antonio Villarreal was the first American of Mexican ancestry to have a novel of Chicano life accepted and brought out by a major publisher. The novel was Pocho, *which came out in 1959. In this excerpt from* Pocho *young Richard Rubio confronts the destructive attitudes that Mexican Americans have historically encountered. Although the excerpt takes place during the years just prior to World War II, it reveals the kind of ethnic consciousness and pride that is associated with the Chicano activists who were to appear two decades later, in the 1960s. The son of a Mexican migrant worker, Villarreal — like his fictional character Richard Rubio — was born and raised in California.*

The world of Richard Rubio was becoming too much for him. He felt that time was going by him in an overly accelerated pace, because he was not aware of days but of weeks and, at times, even months. And he lived in dread that suddenly he should find himself old and ready to die before he could get from life the things it owed him. He was approaching his thirteenth year.

Richard went into the barn that was used to house the town's garbage wagons. Today the barn was empty of equipment and full of young guys and a few older people. Over at one end of the building stood a huge ring. It had two ropes, instead of three, and the posts were big iron pipes wrapped in burlap. There were two kids going at it pretty hard, and suddenly one of them put his hands to his mouth and stood transfixed in the center of the ring. The other one jumped around, throwing punches that either missed his opponent completely or landed on his shoulders or the top of his head. The puncher was too anxious, and the one who couldn't believe his mouth was bleeding got away, and then the bell rang.

Two other guys jumped into the ring then, and started dancing around and flexing like professionals, and then this local guy who was doing pretty good in the game up in the City jumped in there to do the announcing, and another guy who was already in there was the referee.

He noticed that the announcer's face was a little bumpy already and he was already talking through his nose from fighting pro. He was a little guy and he moved around funny — real jerky, like the old silent movies — and somebody said, "There goes the next flyweight champ" — which meant he would be the Filipino champion, since they were the only flyweights around. Richard could tell already he would not even be champ of Santa Clara, but he did not say anything, because people in small towns are funny about things like that — they think they have the best of everything.

While the two guys were fighting, Thomas Nakano came over to him. He was wearing only pants, and they were rolled up to his knees and he was barefooted.

"You gonna fight, Thomas?" asked Ricky.

"I can't find nobody who's my size and wants to fight me," Thomas said, sounding disappointed.

Richard felt his stomach begin to get funny, because he knew what was coming. "Don't look at me, Punchie," he said, trying to make a little joke out of it, but nobody laughed and it was real quiet.

"Aw, come on, Richard." He was begging him to let him hit him. "Come on, you're just my size. I'll fight anybody, only they won't let ya less'n you're the same size as the other guy."

He said no he would not, but he felt sorry for Thomas because he wanted someone to fight with him so bad. And then the guys were finished in the ring, and somebody called Thomas and asked him if he had a partner yet. He said no, but by then even guys Richard didn't know were trying to talk him into fighting him, and the pro came over, and in the end he was up in the ring, shaking, because he didn't want any of these people to see him look bad.

He thought back to the pictures in *Ring Magazine* and tried to imitate the poses, but before he could really decide which he liked best, Thomas was all over him. And Thomas said, "Don't worry — I'll take it easy," and Richard felt pretty good about then, because Thomas was his buddy and he would take it easy on him.

But as they pulled away from each other, Thomas clouted him on the mouth when he wasn't looking, and Richard's head felt suddenly numb. Then Thomas was hitting him all over the place, like nobody's business — in the ribs, the stomach, and even his back sometimes, and the gloves were feeling like great big pillows on Richard's hands. It was the longest round in the history of boxing. *My friend — one of the gang!* So he thought and thought, and finally, when they were apart one time, he dropped his hands and moved toward Thomas, looking real sadlike right into his eyes, as if to say, *Go ahead, kill me.*

Thomas stopped also, and a funny look came to his face, and when Richard knew he was relaxed good, he brought one up from the next neighborhood and clipped him good right on the ear.

Thomas spun clean around and started to walk away; then he walked in a circle and he walked right past Richard and around the other side again, and all Richard could do was stand there and look at the crooked little legs that were browner than his.

Then he heard everybody hollering for him to go after Thomas, and he thought he might as well, so he followed him around, but Thomas wouldn't stand still. So finally he grabbed him and turned him around, and Thomas stood there grinning, and his eyes were almost closed, because his eyelids were almost together anyway. Richard couldn't hit him when he was smiling at him like that. He smiled back at him, and then the bell rang.

Richard couldn't help laughing at Thomas's grin, but suddenly he stopped, because the bell rang again and he knew he was in for it. Right away, Thomas hit him in the stomach, and Richard bent right over, and there it was — he just kept right on going, and landed on his head and took the count there curled up like a fetus. He didn't have to fight any more, and Thomas was very happy as he helped him up, and Thomas kept saying how he was like Fitzsimmons and that his Sunday punch was a right to the solar plexus. "I hit you in the solar plexus, Richard," he said over and over again, but Richard wasn't really listening to him, because he was sneaking looks at the people, and finally decided he had made it look pretty good.

The referee and the professional came over to see him. "Nice faking, kid," said the referee. "How'd ya like to be a fighter?"

"Uh-uh," he said, pulling at the laces with his teeth. The man took his gloves off.

"You don't know how to fight, but you got a punch for a kid and you're smart," he said.

"I not only can't fight, but I'm scared to fight, so you don't want me," he said.

"How old are ya, kid?"

"I'll be thirteen soon."

"I thought you was older," he said. "But I can teach ya a lot, and in a year I can put you in smokers. Make five or ten bucks a night that way."

"Not me, mister. I don't need five or ten bucks."

"How about me?" said Thomas. "I'm the guy that won. You saw me hit him in the solar plexus." Now Richard knew why Thomas had been so anxious to fight.

"Yeah, I can use you, too," said the man, "but I want this other kid."

"Oboyoboy!" said Thomas. He had a trade now.

"How about it, kid?" asked the man. "I'm giving ya the chance of your life— it's the only way people of your nationality can get ahead."

"I'm an American," said Richard.

"All right, you know what I mean. Mexicans don't get too much chance to amount to much. You wanna pick prunes the rest of your life?" Richard didn't say anything, and he said, "Look, I'll go talk it over with your old man, and I'll bet he'll agree with me. I'll bet he knows what's good for you."

"You better not do that, mister. You don't know my old man. He's already been in jail for knifing three guys."

Richard could tell he was dumb and, like a lot of people, believed that Mexicans and knives went together. He thought he had finished with him, but the man said, "All right, we won't tell 'im anything, and when you start bringing money home, he'll come and see *me*."

"Listen," Richard said. "He'll come and see you all right, but it won't make any difference. My old man don't feel about money the way some people do. So leave me alone, why don't you?"

But the man kept insisting, and said, "I gotta line up a smoker for the Eagles, and if you and the Jap kid here put 'em on, I'll give ya each a fin. Then, when your old man sees the dough, he'll be in the bag. What do you say?"

"Okay with me," said Thomas, "but don't call me no Jap." Richard was walking away by then, and the man followed him. "I'll give ya seven-fifty and the Jap a fin."

"No, thanks." He kept walking. They would never be able to make him do anything like that. He was sure he could be no more than a punching bag, because everybody in the neighborhood could beat him, and besides he was afraid.

The guys caught up to him, but he wasn't talking. He thought how funny the guy back there was — the fight manager. He felt that the manager was the kid and he was the grownup. *Amount to something!* Everybody was telling him what he should make of himself these days, and they all had the same argument, except that this guy was thinking of himself. At least the little old lady who was so nice and let him read the Horatio Alger books was thinking of him when she told him he should work hard to be a gardener and someday he could work on a rich person's estate; she was sure he would be successful at that, because she had known of some Mexicans who held very fine places like that. Funny about her, how the Horatio Alger books meant as much to her as the Bible meant to Protestants.

And the adviser in the high school, who had insisted he take auto mechanics or welding or some shop course, so that he could have a trade and be in a position to be a good citizen, because he was Mexican, and when he had insisted on preparing himself for college, she had smiled knowingly and said he could try those courses for a week or so, and she would make an exception and let him change his program to what she knew was better for him. She'd been eating crow ever since. What makes people like that, anyway? Always worried about his being Mexican and he never even thought about it, except sometimes, when he was alone, he got kinda funnyproud about it.

As he walked toward home with the guys, he thought about the things he had just discovered. He would never really be afraid again. Like with hitting Thomas and ending the fight the way he did; funny he had never thought about that before — the alternative. Everything had another way to it, if only you looked hard enough, and he would never be ashamed again for doing something against the unwritten code of honor. Codes of honor were really stupid — it amazed him that he had just learned this — and what people thought was honorable was not important, because he was the important guy. No matter what he did and who was affected by his actions, in the end it came back to him and his feelings. He was himself, and everything else was there because he was *himself*, and it wouldn't be there if he were not himself, and then, of course, it wouldn't matter to him. He had the feeling that *being* was important, and he *was* — so he knew that he would never succumb to foolish social pressures again. And if he hurt anyone, it would be only if he had no choice, for he did not have it in him to hurt willingly.

He thought of Thomas's face in the ring, and began to laugh at the silliness of his grin, and then he laughed louder and louder, about the fight manager and all the people who tried to tell him how to live the good life.

TINO VILLANUEVA

Jugábamos/We Played

One of the most rewarding pleasures in reading literature occurs when familiar experiences are transformed by an imaginative writer who describes them with unexpected awarenesses and startling implications. The process of poetic transformation is well illustrated here, as Tino Villanueva looks back on the boyhood games of a Texas barrio. The theme, cadence, and sensuous details of his poem, as well as the two quotations at the beginning, reveal the author's careful reading of British and American poets, who include his Chicano contemporaries José Montoya and Alurista.

en el barrio
— en las tardes de fuego
when the dusk prowls
    en la calle desierta
pues los jefes y jefas
    trabajan
    — often late hours
after school
    we play canicas. . . .[1]

Alurista

The memories of childhood
have no order, and no end.

Dylan Thomas

we would play/we would jump/
we would play at everything.
ritual and recreation it was, in the patio of my barrio
in the just-awakening week: kneeling there
in sunnybronzed delight
when my kingdom was a pocketful of
golden marbles.
how in wide-eyed wonder i sought winning
two agates for my eyes/& so,
not knowing what it meant, i played for keeps.

***

we would play/we would put our lives on the line —

my posse always got its man/
i was the Chicano Lone Ranger/i was Tarzan
of backyard pecan trees/time-tall trees blooming
with the color of adventure/trees that ripened
with my age through rain-ruined days.

1 *en el barrio . . . canicas* in the barrio/— in the afternoons full of fire/when the dusk prowls/in the deserted street/for our fathers and mothers/work/— often late hours/after school/we play at marbles. . . .

running/gamboling i played oblivious to
fine earth shifting in the cuffs of my fading jeans/
crawling/leaping always reaching/
reaching/reaching even the delicacies of the indomitable
void/
running about the nooks and corners of my patio
where grandma had tulips and carnations planted/
running between the sun and its reverberant glare
in those afternoons of that fire.

***

we would play/we would leap/
we would play at everything.
myth and sensation it was, when the tree-house wind blew
in simultaneous weathers: it was a green wind
tasting of fig, of mint, of peaches at times —

our garden's aromas.

and in my Cracker-Jack-joy of late saturday afternoons
my red wagon was full of dog/& my tricycle traveled
one last time every turnpike of my yard.

now the fun running to soothe the dry sun on my tongue/
now the tireless striding toward stilled water of
buoyant ice cubes in a glass transparent dripping
in the gripping of my mother's hand.

***

we would play/we would run/
we would play at everything.
shouting and emotion it was, in my chosen pastime:

thirteen years out of the womb i was
pubescent Walter Mitty fleet as Mickey Mantle
at the Stadium:

*tok! . . . there's a long drive to center . . . Villanueva
is back/back/back/the ball is up against the wall . . .*

as i banged my back against our dilapidated
picket fence. grandpa repaired it twelve times over.
yes, i dreamed of spikes and baseball diamonds/
meantime
barefooted i played in narrow dusty streets
(a dust decreed by the City Council, i know now.)
my buddies in bubble-gum smiles chose up sides/
so batter up 'cause i'm a portsider like
Whitey Ford/i've the eagle eye of Ted Williams.
i tugged the bill of my sea-blue cap for luck/
had NY on it:

time out! let the dust settle/as it must/
traffic should slow down on gravel streets —

especially Coca-Cola trucks.

but the game goes on/dust mixing with perspiration.
inning after inning this game becomes a night game too/
this 100-watt bulb lights the narrow playing field.

***

such were the times of year-rounded yearnings
when at the end of light's flight i listened in
reflective boyhood silence.
then the day-done sun glistened, burned deeply,
disappearing into my eyes blinking: innocently
i blinked toward the towering twilight.

***

we would play/we would jump/
we would play at everything.

Paris, 2 September 1972

La Causa

The Chicano Movement

mañana doesn't come
    for he who waits
no morrow
    only for he who is now
to whom when equals now
he will see a morrow

Alurista

TINO VILLANUEVA

Day-Long Day

This poem presents a Chicano family in a tragically typical scene. While he creates a sense of the near-suffocating intensity of the Texas sun, the poet also dramatizes the migrant farmworkers' pattern of economic and social deprivation. "Day-Long Day" is from Villanueva's Hay Otra Voz Poems *("There's Another Voice Poems"). The volume contains this dedication: "To my parents — whose multi-weathered fingers, migrant knees, and seasoned backs ripened in cotton fields, and aged on mapless roads to make this possible."*

Again the drag of pisca.[1] pisca
. . pisca . . . Daydreams border
on sun-fed hallucinations, eyes
and hands automatically dis-
criminate whiteness of cotton
from field of vision. Pisca, pisca.

"Un Hijo del Sol,"[2]
Genaro Gonzales

Third-generation timetable.
Sweat day-long dripping into open space;
sun blocks out the sky, suffocates the only breeze.
From el amo desgraciado,[3] a sentence:

"I wanna a bale a day, and the boy here
don't hafta go to school."

1 *pisca* picking cotton 2 *"Un Hijo del Sol"* "A Son of the Sun"
3 *el amo desgraciado* the despicable boss

* * *

In time-binding motion —
a family of sinews and backs,
row-trapped,
zigzagging through summer-long rows
of cotton: Lubbock by way of Wharton.
"Está como si escupieran fuego," [4] a mother moans
in sweat-patched jeans,
stooping
with unbending dreams.
"Estudia para que no seas burro como nosotros," [5]
our elders warn, their gloves and cuffs
leaf-stained by seasons.

* * *

Bronzed and blurry-eyed by
the blast of degrees,
we blend into earth's rotation.
And sweltering toward Saturday, the
day-long day is sunstruck by 6:00 P.M.
One last chug-a-lug from a water jug
old as granddad.
Day-long sweat dripping into open space:
Wharton by way of Lubbock.

4 *"Está . . . fuego."* "It's as if they're spewing fire." 5 *"Estudia . . . nosotros."* "Study so you won't be a dumb beast like us."

Tomás Rivera

When We Arrive

There are probably as many views of a situation as there are people to see it. In this story Tomás Rivera reveals the varied thoughts of some Chicano migrant workers who are being transported by truck from Texas to fields in the North where they will work. Like "A Prayer" (page 89), "When We Arrive" is from the author's bilingual short story collection. Tomás Rivera has taught Spanish and English in schools and colleges.

The truck broke down around four o'clock in the morning. All night they had been hypnotized by the humming of the tires on the pavement. When the truck came to a stop, they awoke. The silence told them that something had happened. The truck had been heating up quite a bit, and when they stopped to examine the motor they found out that it had almost burned out. The truck wouldn't start anymore. They would have to stay there until it became completely daylight and then they could thumb a ride to the nearest town. Inside the truck the people had first awakened, and then several conversations were exchanged back and forth. Then their eyes began to close in the darkness, and everything became so quiet that even the crickets could be heard. Some were asleep; others were thinking.

"*It was a good thing the truck stopped here. I've had a stomachache for quite a while, but by the time I could manage to get to the window and tell them about it I would have had to wake up a great number of people. But one still can't make out anything, almost. I think that the chile I ate didn't agree with me; it was pretty hot and I didn't want to leave it. I hope my wife carrying the baby is all right over there.*"

"*The driver we have this year sure is a good one. He really keeps at it. He doesn't stop for anything. He just gasses up and goes at it again. We've been on the road more than twenty-four hours. We should be close to Des Moines. I'd sure like to sit down, at least for a little while. I'd get down and lie down by the road, but one can never tell if there might be a snake or some other animal. Before falling asleep on my feet I felt my knees buckle, although I think that the body gets used to it right away, because it isn't so hard for me anymore. The children must really get tired traveling up on their feet like that. Nothing to hold on to. We grownups can at least hold on to the center bar that holds up the canvas. But the fact is that we're not as cramped this time as we have been other times. I think we have forty people at the very most. I remember once, the time I traveled with a bunch of wetbacks, there were more than seventy of us. One couldn't even smoke."*

"The Negro was sure shocked when I ordered those fifty-four hamburgers at two o'clock in the morning. I had entered the restaurant all alone, and probably he didn't see the truck full of people. 'At two o'clock in the morning, hamburgers? Fifty-four of them? Man, you must eat a lot.' The fact was that the people hadn't eaten and the driver said, in order not to delay so long and waste so much time, that only one person should get down and order for everyone. The Negro was really shocked. He couldn't believe what I had ordered. That I wanted fifty-four hamburgers. At two o'clock in the morning, if one is hungry, one can very well eat all those hamburgers."

"This is the last year I come over here. Just as soon as we get to the ranch I'll get out of here. I'm going to look for a job in Minneapolis. It's easier to make a living. I'll look up my uncle; maybe he'll get me a job at the hotel where he works as a bellboy. Maybe they'll give me a break there, or at some other hotel."

"If things go well for us this year, maybe we can buy a car so we won't have to travel like cattle. My girls are pretty big now, and they already feel embarrassment. Sometimes the garages have some good buys. I'll discuss it with my compadre; he already knows the car salesmen. I'll get one I

really like even if it's an old secondhand car. I'm tired of coming over here in a truck. My compadre took back a good car last year. If we do all right in the onion harvest, I'll buy one that's at least halfway decent. I'll teach my son to drive and he can drive it all the way to Texas. And I hope he doesn't get lost like my nephew; they wound up in New Mexico just because they wouldn't stop to ask for directions. If not, I can ask Mundo to drive it and I won't charge him for the trip. We'll see if he agrees."

"With the money that Mr. Thompson loaned us we can eat for at least three months. By that time we'll have the money from working in the beets. I hope we don't get too much in debt. He loaned me two hundred dollars, but by the time one pays for the trip almost half of it is gone, what with this business of having to pay half fare for children. And when I get back I have to pay back double the amount. Four hundred dollars! Interest is too high, but there's no way out of it; one can't fool around when one is in need. I've been told to turn him in because the interest rates are too high, but the fact is that he even has the trust deed to my house already. I sure hope everything goes well for us in the beet harvest; if not we'll be left homeless. We'll have to save enough to pay him back the four hundred dollars. Maybe there'll be something after that. And the kids have to go to school now. I don't know; I hope everything turns out all right for us; if not, I don't know what we're going to do. I just pray to God that there's work for us."

"This is the last time I travel like an animal, standing up all the way. Just as soon as we arrive I'm going to Minneapolis; surely I'll find something to do there where I don't have to work like an animal. That's what I get for being stupid."

"My poor husband, he must be very tired by now, standing all the way. And there's no way I can help him, burdened as I am with the two children I'm holding. I wish we had already arrived, so we could lie down even on a hard floor. Children are sure a lot of work. I wish I could help

him out in the fields this year, but I think that this year, with the kids, I won't be able to do anything. I'll have to breastfeed them every little while, and also they're still so little. I wish they were a little older. But I'll do my best to help him. At least I can help him along in his row so he won't feel the strain so much. Even if it's just at short intervals. That husband of mine, from the time the kids are still small he already wants them to be in school. I hope I can help him. May God grant that I be able to help him."

"The stars look good from here. It almost seems as though they actually come down to touch the canvas on the truck. There doesn't seem to be anyone inside. There's almost no traffic at this hour. A trailer goes by once in a while. The dawn's silence makes everything appear so smooth. Wouldn't it be better if it were always dawn? We'll be here until noon for sure. By the time they get help in town and then by the time they fix the motor. If dawn would only stay, no one would say anything. I'm going to watch the sky until the last star disappears. I wonder how many others are looking at the same star. Everything is so quiet that it makes me think that the crickets are talking to the stars."

"It's a constant hassle with this truck. When we get there the people will have to get along as best they can. I'm just going to distribute them among the growers and get out of there. Furthermore, we've never signed any contract. They'll find someone to take them back to Texas; someone will come along and pick them up for sure. There's no money in beets anymore. The best thing for me to do is go back to Texas as soon as I drop these people off, and then I'll see how I make out hauling watermelons. The watermelon harvest will be here soon. What if there's no one in this town who can fix the truck? That's all I need. Then what do I do? Just as long as the cops don't come and hassle me to move the truck away from here. In that other town we didn't even stop, but nevertheless the cops came up to us and told us they didn't want us to stay there. I think they just wanted to look good in front of the townspeople. We didn't even stop in their town. When we arrive, and as soon

as I parcel them out among the growers, I'll head right back. Let each one look out for his own skin."

"When we arrive I'll see if I can find a good bed for my wife; her kidneys are really bothering her. I hope we don't wind up in a chicken coop with a cement floor, as we did last year. Even covering the floor with straw didn't help because as soon as the cold weather settled in, it became unbearable. I'm sure that's why my rheumatism hit me hard."

"When we arrive, when we arrive. At this point, quite frankly, I'm tired of always arriving someplace. Arriving is the same as leaving, because as soon as we arrive . . . well, quite frankly, I'm tired of always arriving. Maybe I should say when we don't arrive, because that's the plain truth. We never really arrive anywhere."

"When we arrive, when we arrive. . . ."

Little by little the crickets ended their chirping. It seemed as though they were getting tired, and the light of dawn began to verify the existence of different objects very carefully, very slowly, so that no one would realize what was happening. The people once again became people. They started to get out of the truck and huddled around. They started to talk about what they would do when they arrived.

CÉSAR CHÁVEZ

The Organizer's Tale

Although César Chávez and his union of farmworkers first received national attention during the Delano strike of 1965, Chávez's own struggle and that of farm laborers in California had begun long before. Born in Arizona, César Chávez spent some years as a migrant worker before settling with his family in San Jose, California. There he gradually emerged as an important labor leader. As Chávez recalls the early years, he reveals how someone with little formal education learned the skills of social organization and leadership. This article was written during the strike at Delano.

It really started for me sixteen years ago in San Jose, California, when I was working on an apricot farm. We figured he was just another social worker doing a study of farm conditions, and I kept refusing to meet with him. But he was persistent. Finally, I got together some of the rough element in San Jose. We were going to have a little reception for him to teach the gringo a little bit of how we felt. There were about thirty of us in the house, young guys mostly. I was supposed to give them a signal — change my cigarette from my right hand to my left. But he started talking and the more he talked, the more wide-eyed I became and the less inclined I was to give the signal. A couple of guys who were pretty drunk at the time still wanted to give the gringo the business, but we got rid of them. This fellow was making a lot of sense, and I wanted to hear what he had to say.

His name was Fred Ross, and he was an organizer for the Community Service Organization (CSO), which was working with Mexican Americans in the cities. I became immediately really involved. Before long I was heading a voter-registration drive. All the time I was observing the things Fred did, secretly, because I wanted to learn how to organize, to see how it was done. I was impressed with his patience and understanding of people. I thought this was a tool, one of the greatest things he had.

It was pretty rough for me at first. I was changing and had to take a lot of ridicule from the kids my age, the rough characters I worked with in the fields. They would say, "Hey, big shot. Now that you're a político, why are you working here for sixty-five cents an hour?" I might add that our neighborhood had the highest percentage of San Quentin graduates. It was a game among the pachucos in the sense that we defended ourselves from outsiders, although inside the neighborhood there was not a lot of fighting.

After six months of working every night in San Jose, Fred assigned me to take over the CSO chapter in Decoto. It was a tough spot to fill. I would suggest something, and people would say, "No, let's wait till Fred gets back" or "Fred wouldn't do it that way." This is pretty much a pattern with people, I discovered, whether I was put in Fred's position or, later, when someone else was put in my position. After the Decoto assignment I was sent to start a new chapter in Oakland. Before I left, Fred came to a place in San Jose called the Hole-in-the-Wall and we talked for half an hour over coffee. He was in a rush to leave, but I wanted to keep him talking; I was that scared of my assignment.

Those were hard times in Oakland. First of all, it was a big city and I'd get lost every time I went anywhere. Then I arranged a series of house meetings. I would get to the meeting early and drive back and forth past the house, too nervous to go in and face the people. Finally I would force myself to go inside and sit in a corner. I was quite thin then, and young, and most of the people were middle-aged. Someone would say, "Where's the organizer?" And I would pipe up, "Here I am." Then they would say in Spanish — these were very poor people and we hardly spoke anything but Spanish — "Ha! This *kid?*" Most of them said they were interested, but the hardest part was to get them to start pushing themselves, on their own initiative.

The idea was to set up a meeting and then get each attending person to call his own house meeting, inviting new people — a sort of chain-letter effect. After a house meeting

I would lie awake going over the whole thing, playing the tape back, trying to see why people laughed at one point or why they were for one thing and against another. I was also learning to read and write, those late evenings. I had left school in the seventh grade after attending sixty-seven different schools, and my reading wasn't the best.

At our first organizing meeting we had 368 people; I'll never forget it because it was very important to me. You eat your heart out; the meeting is called for seven o'clock and you start to worry about four. You wait. Will they show up? Then the first one arrives. By seven there are only twenty people; you have everything in order, you have to look calm. But little by little they filter in, and at a certain point you know it will be a success.

After four months in Oakland, I was transferred. The chapter was beginning to move on its own, so Fred assigned me to organize the San Joaquin Valley. Over the months I developed what I used to call schemes or tricks — now I call them techniques — of making initial contacts. The main thing in convincing someone is to spend time with him. It doesn't matter if he can read, write, or even speak well. What is important is that he is a man and, second, that he has shown some initial interest. One good way to develop leadership is to take a man with you in your car. And it works a lot better if you're doing the driving; that way you are in charge. You drive, he sits there, and you talk. These little things were very important to me; I was caught in a big game by then, figuring out what makes people work. I found that if you work hard enough, you can usually shake people into working too, those who are concerned. You work harder and they work harder still — up to a point, and then they pass you. Then, of course, they're on their own.

I also learned to keep away from the established groups and so-called leaders, and to guard against philosophizing. Working with low-income people is very different from working with the professionals, who like to sit around talking about how to play politics. When you're trying to recruit a farmworker, you have to paint a little picture, and then you have to color the picture in. We found out that the harder a guy is to convince, the better leader or member he becomes. When you exert yourself to convince him, you have his confidence and he has good motivation. A lot of people who say OK right away wind up hanging around the office, taking up the workers' time.

During the McCarthy[1] era in one Valley town, I was subjected to a lot of red-baiting. We had been recruiting people for citizenship classes at the high school when we got into a quarrel with the naturalization examiner. He was rejecting people on the grounds that they were just parroting what they learned in citizenship class. One day we had a meeting about it in Fresno, and I took along some of the leaders of our local chapter. Some red-baiting official gave us a hard time, and the people got scared and took his side. They did it because it seemed easy at the moment, even though they knew that sticking with me was the right thing to do. It was disgusting. When we left the building, they walked by themselves ahead of me as if I had some kind of communicable disease. I had been working with these people for three months and I was very sad to see that. It taught me a great lesson.

That night I learned that the chapter officers were holding a meeting to review my letters and printed materials to see if I really was a Communist. So I drove out there and walked right in on their meeting. I said, "I hear you've been discussing me, and I thought it would be nice if I was here to defend myself. Not that it matters that much to you or even to me, because as far as I'm concerned you are a bunch of cowards." At that they began to apologize. "Let's forget it," they said. "You're a nice guy."

But I didn't want apologies. I wanted a full discussion. I told them that they had to learn to distinguish fact from what appeared to be a fact because of fear. I kept them there till two in the morning. Some of the women cried. I don't know if they investigated me any further, but I stayed on another few months and things worked out.

1 *McCarthy* a reference to the late Senator Joseph McCarthy, chairman of the Permanent Subcommittee on Investigations, who in the mid-1950s conducted 157 inquiries to uncover cases of subversive activity or disloyalty, mostly among government employees.

This was not an isolated case. Often when we'd leave people to themselves, they would get frightened and draw back into their shells where they had been all the years. And I learned quickly that there is no real appreciation. Whatever you do, and no matter what reasons you may give to others, you do it because you want to see it done, or maybe because you want power. And there shouldn't be any appreciation, understandably. I know good organizers who were destroyed, washed out, because they expected people to appreciate what they'd done. Things don't work that way.

For more than ten years I worked for the CSO. As the organization grew, we found ourselves meeting in fancier and fancier motels and holding expensive conventions. Doctors, lawyers, and politicians began joining. They would get elected to some office in the organization and then, for all practical purposes, leave. Intent on using the CSO for their own prestige purposes, these "leaders," many of them, lacked the urgency we had to have. When I became general director, I began to press for a program to organize farmworkers into a union — an idea most of the leadership opposed. So I started a revolt within the CSO. I refused to sit at the head table at meetings, refused to wear a suit and tie, and finally I even refused to shave and cut my hair. It used to embarrass some of the professionals.

At every meeting I got up and gave my standard speech: we shouldn't meet in fancy motels, we were getting away from the people, farmworkers had to be organized. But nothing happened. In March of '62 I resigned and came to Delano to begin organizing the Valley on my own.

I drew a map of all the towns between Arvin and Stockton — eighty-six of them, including farming camps — and decided to hit them all to get a small nucleus of people working in each. For six months I traveled around, planting an idea. We had a simple questionnaire, a little card with space for name, address, and how much the worker thought he ought to be paid. My wife, Helen, mimeographed them, and we took our kids for two- or three-day jaunts to these towns, distributing the cards door to door and to camps and groceries.

Some eighty thousand cards were sent back from eight Valley counties. I got a lot of contacts that way, but I was shocked at the wages the people were asking. The growers were paying $1.00 and $1.15, and maybe 95 percent of the people thought they should be getting only $1.25. Sometimes people scribbled messages on the cards: "I hope to God we win" or "Do you think we can win?" or "I'd like to know more." So I separated the cards with the penciled notes, got in my car, and went to those people.

We didn't have any money at all in those days, none for gas and hardly any for food. So I went to people and started asking for food. It turned out to be about the best thing I could have done, although at first it's hard on your pride. Some of our best members came in that way. If people give you their food, they'll give you their hearts. Several months and many meetings later we had a working organization, and this time the leaders were the people.

None of the farmworkers had collective bargaining contracts, and I thought it would take ten years before we got that first contract. I wanted desperately to get some color into the movement, to give people something they could identify with, like a flag. I was reading some books about how various leaders discovered what colors contrasted and stood out the best. The Egyptians had found that a red field with a white circle and a black emblem in the center crashed into your eyes like nothing else. I wanted to use the Aztec eagle in the center, as on the Mexican flag. So I told my cousin Manuel, "Draw an Aztec eagle." Manuel had a little trouble with it, so we modified the eagle to make it easier for people to draw.

The first big meeting of what we decided to call the National Farm Workers Association was held in September 1962, at Fresno, with 287 people. We had our huge red flag on the wall, with paper tacked over it. When the time came, Manuel pulled a cord, ripping the paper off the flag, and all of a sudden it hit the people. Some of them wondered if it was a Communist flag, and I said it probably looked more like a neo-Nazi emblem than anything else. But they wanted an explanation, so Manuel got up and said, "When that eagle flies — that's when the farmworkers' problems are going to be solved."

One of the first things I decided was that outside money wasn't going to organize people, at least not in the beginning. I even turned down a grant from a private group — $50,000 to go directly to organize farmworkers — for just this reason. Even when there are no strings attached, you are still compromised because you feel you have to produce immediate results. This is bad, because it takes a long time to build a movement, and your organization suffers if you get too far ahead of the people it belongs to. We set the dues at $42 a year per family — really meaningful dues — but of the 212 families we got to pay, only twelve remained by June of '63. We were discouraged at that, but not enough to make us quit.

Money was always a problem. Once we were facing a $180 gas bill on a credit card I'd got a long time ago and was about to lose. And we *had* to keep that credit card.

One day my wife and I were picking cotton, pulling bolls, to make a little money to live on. Helen said to me, "Do you put all this in the bag, or just the cotton?" I thought she was kidding and told her to throw the whole boll in, so that she had nothing but a sack of bolls at the weighing.

The man said, "Whose sack is this?" I said, "Well, my wife's," and he told us we were fired.

Helen and I started laughing. We were going anyway. We took the $4 we had earned and spent it at a grocery store where they were giving away a $100 prize. Each time you shopped they'd give you one of the letters of M-O-N-E-Y or a flag; you had to have M-O-N-E-Y plus the flag to win. Helen had already collected the letters and just needed the flag. Anyway, they gave her the ticket. She screamed, "A flag? I don't believe it," ran in, and got the $100. She said, "Now we're going to eat steak." But I said, "No, we're going to pay the gas bill." I don't know if she cried, but I think she did.

It was rough in those early years. Helen was having babies and I was not there when she was at the hospital.

But if you haven't got your wife behind you, you can't do many things. There's got to be peace at home. So I did, I think, a fairly good job of organizing her. When we were kids, she lived in Delano and I came to town as a migrant. Once on a date we had a bad experience about segregation at a movie theater, and I put up a fight. We were together then, and still are. I think I'm more of a pacifist than she is. Her father, Fabela, was a colonel with Pancho Villa in the Mexican Revolution. Sometimes she gets angry and tells me, "These scabs — you should deal with them sternly," and I kid her, "It must be too much of that Fabela blood in you."

The Movement really caught on in '64. By August we had a thousand members. We'd had a beautiful ninety-day drive in Corcoran, where they had the Battle of the Corcoran Farm Camp thirty years ago, and by November we had assets of $25,000 in our credit union, which helped to stabilize the membership. I had gone without pay the whole of 1963. The next year the members voted me a $40-a-week salary, after Helen had to quit working in the fields to manage the credit union.

Our first strike was in May of '65 — a small one but it prepared us for the big one. A farmworker from McFarland named Epifanio Camacho came to see me. He said he was sick and tired of how people working the roses were being treated, and was willing to "go the limit."

I assigned Manuel and Gilbert Padilla to hold meetings at Camacho's house. The people wanted union recognition, but the real issue, as in most cases when you begin, was wages. They were promised $9.00 a thousand, but they were actually getting $6.50 and $7.00 for grafting roses. Most of them signed cards giving us the right to bargain for them. We chose the biggest company, with about eighty-five employees, not counting the irrigators and supervisors, and we held a series of meetings to prepare the strike and call the vote. There would be no picket line; everyone pledged on their honor not to break the strike.

Early on the first morning of the strike, we sent out ten cars to check the people's homes. We found lights in five or six homes and knocked on the doors. The men were getting up, and we'd say, "Where are you going?" They would dodge. "Oh, uh . . . I was just getting up, you know." We'd say, "Well, you're not going to work, are you?" And they'd say no. Dolores Huerta, who was driving the green panel truck, saw a light in one house where four rose workers lived. They told her they were going to work, even after she reminded them of their pledge. So she moved the truck so it blocked their driveway, turned off the key, put it in her purse, and sat there alone.

That morning the company foreman refused to talk to us. None of the grafters had shown up for work. At 10:30 we started to go to the company office, but it occurred to us that maybe a woman would have a better chance. So Dolores knocked on the office door, saying, "I'm Dolores Huerta from the National Farm Workers Association."

"Get out!" the man said. "You Communist. Get out!" I guess they were expecting us, because as Dolores stood arguing with him the cops came and told her to leave. She left.

For two days the fields were idle. On Wednesday they recruited a group of Filipinos from out of town who knew nothing of the strike, maybe thirty-five of them. They drove through escorted by three sheriff's patrol cars — one in front, one in the middle, and one at the rear with a dog. We didn't have a picket line, but we parked across the street and just watched them go through, not saying a word. All but seven stopped working after half an hour, and the rest had quit by midafternoon.

The company made an offer the evening of the fourth day, a package deal that amounted to a 120-percent wage increase, but no contract. We wanted to hold out for a contract and more benefits, but a majority of the rose workers wanted to accept the offer and go back. We are a democratic union, so we had to support what they wanted to do. They had a meeting and voted to settle. Then we had a problem with a few militants who wanted to hold out. We had to convince them to go back to work, as a united front, because otherwise they could be canned. So we worked —

Tony Orendain and I, Dolores and Gilbert, Jim Drake and all the organizers — knocking on doors till two in the morning, telling people, "You have to go back or you'll lose your job."

And they did. They worked.

Our second strike, and our last before the big one at Delano, was in the grapes at Martin's Ranch. The people were getting a raw deal there, being pushed around pretty badly. Gilbert went out to the field, climbed on top of a car, and took a strike vote. They voted unanimously to go out. Right away they started bringing in strikebreakers, so we launched a tough attack on the labor contractors, distributed leaflets portraying them as really low characters. We attacked one so badly that he just gave up the job, and he took twenty-seven of his men out with him. All he asked was that we distribute another leaflet reinstating him in the community. And we did. What was unusual was that the grower would still talk to us. The grower kept saying, "I can't pay. I just haven't got the money." I guess he must have found the money somewhere, because we were asking $1.40 and we got it.

We had just finished the Martin strike when the Agricultural Workers Organizing Committee (AFL-CIO) started a strike against the grape growers, DiGiorgio, Schenley liquors, and small growers, asking $1.40 an hour and 25 cents a box. There was a lot of pressure from our members for us to join the strike, but we had some misgivings. We didn't feel ready for a big strike like this one, one that was sure to last a long time. Having no money — just $87 in the strike fund — meant we'd have to depend on God knows who.

Eight days after the strike started — it takes time to get twelve hundred people together from all over the Valley — we held a meeting in Delano and voted to go out. I asked the membership to release us from the pledge not to accept outside money, because we'd need it now, a lot of it. The help came. It started because of the close, and I would say even beautiful, relationship that we've had with the Migrant Ministry for some years. They were the first to come to our rescue, financially and in every other way, and they spread the word to other benefactors.

We had planned, before, to start a labor school in November. It never happened, but we have the best labor school we could ever have, in the strike. The strike is only a temporary condition, however. We have over three thousand members spread out over a wide area, and we have to service them when they have problems. We get letters from New Mexico, Colorado, Texas, California, from farmworkers saying, "We're getting together and we need an organizer."

It kills you when you haven't got the personnel and resources. You feel badly about not sending an organizer because you look back and remember all the difficulty you had in getting two or three people together, and here *they're* together. Of course, we're training organizers, many of them younger than I was when I started in CSO. They can work twenty hours a day, sleep four, and be ready to hit it again; when you get to be thirty-nine it's a different story.

The people who took part in the strike and the march have something more than their material interest going for them. If it were only material, they wouldn't have stayed on the strike long enough to win. It is difficult to explain. But it flows out in the ordinary things they say. For instance, some of the younger guys are saying, "Where do you think's going to be the next strike?"

I say, "Well, we have to win in Delano."

They say, "We'll win, but where do we go next?"

I say, "Maybe most of us will be working in the fields."

They say, "No, I don't want to go and work in the fields. I want to organize. There are a lot of people that need our help."

So I say, "You're going to be pretty poor then, because when you strike you don't have much money." They say they don't care much about that.

And others are saying, "I have friends who are working in Texas. If we could only help them."

It is bigger, certainly, than just a strike. And if this spirit grows within the farm labor movement, one day we can use the force that we have to help correct a lot of things that are wrong in this society. But that is for the future. Before you can run, you have to learn to walk.

There are vivid memories from my childhood — what we had to go through because of low wages and the conditions, basically because there was no union. I suppose if I wanted to be fair, I could say that I'm trying to settle a personal score. I could dramatize it by saying that I want to bring social justice to farmworkers. But the truth is that I went through a lot of hell, and a lot of people did. If we can even the score a little for the workers, then we are doing something. Besides, I don't know any other work I like to do better than this. I really don't, you know.

Enriqueta Longeaux y Vásquez

The Woman of La Raza

Some women welcome the concept of a universal "sisterhood," but others — especially some minority women — are hesitant to ally themselves with the women's movement as a whole. They are disturbed by the fact that the energies of some in this movement have concentrated on "male chauvinism" as the only villain. In this essay a Colorado-born writer tries to explain the reasons for the Chicana's allegiance to her male counterpart. At the same time, she relates the history and clarifies the goals of Chicana feminism. Known to some readers as a journalist and to others as a poet, Enriqueta Longeaux y Vásquez is the co-author of Viva La Raza!, *a history of the Chicano movement.*

While attending a Mexican American conference in Colorado this year, I went to one of the workshops that were held to discuss the role of the Chicana — the Mexican American woman, the woman of La Raza. When the time came for the women to report to the full conference, the only thing that the workshop representative had to say was this: "It was the consensus of the group that the Chicana woman does not want to be liberated."

As a woman who has been faced with living as a member of the Mexican American minority group, as a breadwinner and a mother raising children, living in housing projects, and having much concern for other humans plus much community involvement, I felt this as quite a blow. I could have cried. Surely we could at least have come up with something to add to that statement. I sat back and thought, Why? Why? Then I understood why the statement had been made, and I realized that going along with the feelings of the men at the convention was perhaps the best thing to do at the time.

Looking at the history of the Chicana or Mexican woman, we see that her role has been a very strong one — although a silent one. When the woman has seen the suffering of her people, she has always responded bravely and as a totally committed and equal human. My mother told me of how, during the time of Pancho Villa and the revolution in Mexico, she saw the men march through the village continually for three days and then she saw the battalion of women marching for a whole day. The women carried food and supplies; also, they were fully armed and wearing loaded carrilleras.[1] In battle they fought alongside the men. Out of the Mexican Revolution came the revolutionary personage Adelita, who wore her rebozo[2] crossed at the bosom as a symbol of the revolutionary women in Mexico.

Then we have our heroine Juana Gallo, a brave woman who led her men to battle against the government after having seen her father and other villagers hung for defending the land of the people. She and many other women fought bravely with their people. And if called upon again, they would be there alongside the men to fight to the bitter end.

Today, as we hear the call of La Raza and as the dormant, "docile" Mexican American comes to life, we see again the stirring of the people. With that call the Chicana woman also stirs, and I am sure that she will leave her mark upon the Mexican American movement in the Southwest.

How the Chicana woman reacts depends totally on how the macho Chicano is treated when he goes out into the mainstream of society. If the husband is so-called successful, the woman seems to become very domineering and demands more and more in material goods. I ask myself at times, Why are the women so demanding? Can they not see what they make of their men? But then I realize: this is the price of owning a slave.

A woman who has no way of expressing herself and of realizing herself as a full human has nothing else to turn to but the owning of material things. She builds her entire life

1 *carrilleras* cartridge belts
2 *rebozo* shawl

around these and finds security in this way. All she has to live for is her house and family; she becomes very possessive of both. This makes her a totally dependent human. Dependent on her husband and family. Most of the Chicana women in this comfortable situation are not particularly involved in the Movement. Many times it is because of the fear of censorship in general. Censorship from the husband, the family, friends, and society in general. For these reasons she is completely inactive.

Then you will find the Chicana whose husband was not able to fare so very well in society and perhaps has had to face defeat. This is the Chicana who really suffers. Quite often the man will not fight the real source of his problems, be it discrimination or whatever, but will instead come home and take it out on his family. As this continues, his Chicana becomes the victim of his machismo, and woeful are the trials and tribulations of that household.

Much of this is seen, particularly in the city. The man, being head of the household but unable to fight the system he lives in, will very likely lose face and for this reason there will often be a separation or divorce in a family. It is at this time that the Chicana faces the real test of having to confront society as one of its total victims.

There are many things she must do. She must 1) find a way to feed and clothe the family, 2) find housing, 3) find employment, 4) provide child care, and 5) find some kind of social outlet and friendship.

1) In order to find a way to feed and clothe her family, she must find a job. Because of her suppression she has probably not been able to develop a skill. She is probably unable to find a job that will pay her a decent wage. If she is able to find a job at all, it will probably be sought only for survival. Thus she can hope just to exist; she will hardly be able to live an enjoyable life. Here one of the most difficult problems for the Chicana woman to face is that of going to work. Even if she does have a skill, she must all at once realize that she has been living in a racist society. She will have much difficulty in proving herself in any position. Her work must be three times as good as that of the Anglo majority. Not only this, but the competitive way of the

Anglo will always be there. The Anglo woman is always there with her superiority complex. The Chicana woman will be looked upon as having to prove herself even in the smallest task. She is constantly being put to the test. Not only does she suffer the oppression that the Anglo woman suffers as a woman in the market of humanity, but she must also suffer the oppression of being a minority person with a different set of values. Because her existence and the livelihood of the children depend on her conforming, she tries very hard to conform. Thus she may find herself even rejecting herself as a Mexican American. Existence itself depends on this.

2) She must find housing that she will be able to afford. She will very likely be unable to live in a decent place; it will be more the matter of finding a place that is cheap. It is likely that she will have to live in a housing project. Here she will be faced with the real problem of trying to raise children in an environment that is conducive to much suffering. The decision as to where she will live is a difficult matter, as she must come face to face with making decisions entirely on her own. This, plus having to live them out, is very traumatic for her.

3) In finding a job she will be faced with working very hard during the day and coming home to an empty house and again having to work at home. Cooking, washing, ironing, mending, plus spending some time with the children. Her role changes to being both father and mother. All of this, plus being poor, is very hard to bear. On top of this, to have a survey worker or social worker tell you that you have to have incentive and motivations — these are tough pressures to live under. Few men could stand up under such pressures.

4) Child care is one of the most difficult problems for a woman to have to face alone. Not only is she tormented with having to leave the raising of her children to someone else, but she wants the best of care for them. For the amount of money that she may be able to pay from her meager wages, it is likely that she will be lucky to find anyone at all to take care of the children. The routine of the household is not normal at all. She must start her day earlier than an

average worker. She must clothe and feed the children before she takes them to be cared for in someone else's home. Then, too, she will have a very hard day at work, for she is constantly worrying about the children. If there are medical problems, this will only multiply her stress during the day. Not to mention the financial pressure of medical care.

5) With all of this, the fact still remains that she is a human and must have some kind of friendship and entertainment in life, and this is perhaps one of the most difficult tasks facing the Mexican American woman alone. She can probably enjoy very little entertainment, since she cannot afford a babysitter. This, plus the fact that she very likely does not have the clothes, transportation, etc. As she cannot afford entertainment herself, she may very often fall prey to letting someone else pay for her entertainment and this may create unwanted involvement with some friend. When she begins to keep company with men, she will meet with the disapproval of her family and often be looked upon as having loose moral values. As quite often she is not free to remarry in the eyes of the Church, she will find more and more conflict and disapproval, and she continues to look upon herself with guilt and censorship. Thus she suffers much as a human. Everywhere she looks she seems to be rejected.

This woman has much to offer the movement of the Mexican American. She has had to live all of the roles of her Raza. She has had to suffer the torments of her people in that she has had to go out into a racist society and be a provider as well as a mother. She has been doubly oppressed and is trying very hard to find a place. Because of all this, she is a very, very strong individual. She has had to become strong in order to exist against these odds.

The Mexican American movement is not that of just adults fighting the social system, but it is a total commitment of a family unit living what it believes to be a better way of life in demanding social change for the benefit of humankind. When a family is involved in a human rights movement, as is the Mexican American family, there is little room for a woman's liberation movement alone. There is little room for having a definition of woman's role as such. Roles are for actors, and the business at hand requires people living the examples of social change. The Mexican American movement demands are such that, with the liberation of La Raza, we must have a total liberation. The woman must help liberate the man and the man must look upon this liberation with the woman at his side — not behind him, following, but alongside of him, leading. The family must come up together.

The Raza movement is based on brother- and sisterhood. We must look at each other as one large family. We must look at all of the children as belonging to all of us. We must strive for the fulfillment of all as equals, with the full capability and right to develop as humans. When a man can look upon a woman as human, then and only then can he feel the true meaning of liberation and equality.

ABELARDO DELGADO

stupid america

Sometimes a poet jolts his readers to attention by taunting them. With his repeated first line and with a careful structure of examples and details Abelardo Delgado moves the reader along to the unforgettable closing lines, which disturb with their tragedy and truth. Abelardo, as he is usually known, was born in Mexico but came to live in Texas in 1943. Presently on the faculty at the University of Utah, he has worked as a community organizer and has written extensively.

stupid america, see that chicano
with a big knife
in his steady hand
he doesn't want to knife you
he wants to sit on a bench
and carve christ figures
but you won't let him.
stupid america, hear that chicano
shouting curses on the street
he is a poet
without paper and pencil
and since he cannot write
he will explode.
stupid america, remember that chicanito
flunking math and english
he is the picasso
of your western states
but he will die
with one thousand masterpieces
hanging only from his mind.

RUBÉN SALAZAR

Stranger in One's Land

A Mexican-born Californian, Rubén Salazar was both a columnist for the Los Angeles Times *and the news director of station KMEX–TV. As a journalist he articulated the problems and frustrations of Chicanos in the Los Angeles area. Salazar never advocated violence. Ironically, he himself fell victim to violence on August 29, 1970, when he was killed by a tear gas projectile during a peace rally that resulted in a mass confrontation between Chicanos and police. Four months earlier, "Stranger in One's Land" had appeared as the introduction to a government publication on the December 1968 hearing of the U.S. Commission on Civil Rights in San Antonio.*

The San Antonio hearing of the U.S. Commission on Civil Rights which probed into the social anguish of Mexican Americans was born in protest and began in controversy.

As the country's second largest minority, Mexican Americans had been virtually ignored by public and private reformers. There was vague realization that they had educational, employment, and cultural problems. But it was felt that language was the basic reason for these problems. And, it was concluded, once this accident of birth was repaired, Mexican Americans would melt into the Caucasian pot, just as Italians, Germans, and Poles had.

Then came the black revolution.

It exploded partly from a condition which had been known all along but was now the basis for a black-white confrontation: the color of one's skin was all too important in America. White was good. Black was bad.

Faced with an identity crisis, many young Mexican Americans — excited by black militancy — decided that they had been misled by their elders into apathetic confusion. It came as a shock at first: Mexican Americans felt caught between the white and the black. Though counted as "white" by the Bureau of the Census, Mexican Americans were never really thought of as such. Though the speaking of foreign languages was considered highly sophisticated, Mexican Americans were condemned for speaking Spanish.

The ambivalence felt vaguely and in silence for so long seemed to crystallize in the light of the black revolution. A Mexican American was neither Mexican nor American. He was neither white nor black. What was he, then, and where was he going? The young, the militant, and the angry wanted to know.

When the Commission met in San Francisco in May 1967, Mexican Americans walked out protesting there was not a Mexican American Commissioner to represent them or enough attention accorded their problems.

In October of that year, the U.S. Inter-Agency Committee on Mexican American Affairs held a hearing in El Paso on the problems of the Spanish-speaking. The hearing, conducted at the same time President Johnson officially returned to Mexico a disputed piece of border land [El Chamizal], ended on a sour note.

Governor John Connally of Texas, accused of allowing the use of Texas Rangers to break strikes by Mexican American farm workers in the Rio Grande Valley, was roundly booed and hooted by Mexican Americans in the presence of President Johnson. Because the President was there, the incident was given wide publicity and it marked a rare national exposure of rising Mexican American militancy.

In other areas of the Southwest, the strike-boycott of California table grapes led by César Chávez was becoming a national and international cause. Reies López Tijerina's land grants struggle in New Mexico and its adversaries introduced violence to the movement. There were the high school walkouts in East Los Angeles by Mexican American students, and Rodolfo (Corky) Gonzales, head of the Denver-based Crusade for Justice, was preaching ethnic nationalism. Many Mexican Americans joined the Poor People's Campaign in Washington, D.C., in the summer of 1968.

For the first time, many Americans became aware of Mexican American discontent. There was talk now of brown power.

In November 1968, President Johnson named the first Mexican American to the Commission, Dr. Hector P. García, a physician from Corpus Christi, Texas, and founder of the American G.I. Forum. A Commission hearing which would center on Mexican American problems was scheduled for December 9–14, in San Antonio.

Protests helped bring it about. Now the controversy would begin.

Some Mexican American leaders charged that Washington was meddling in something it knew nothing about and so would make things worse instead of better. They felt any problems Mexican Americans might have should be solved locally, by local leadership. The younger and the more militant Chicano leadership retorted that the problems had intentionally been ignored and that national exposure would bring new, more imaginative solutions. Traditional leadership, they claimed, had failed.

These strong points of view, aired publicly before the Commission met, hint at the diversity of thought and feeling found among the some six to seven million Mexican Americans, most of whom live in California, Texas, New Mexico, Arizona, and Colorado.

There are many splits in the black movement. But there's something the American Negro knows for sure — he's black. He can easily define his problems as a race which make him part of a cohesive force. This is what has forged the beginning of black power in the United States. As yet, most Mexican Americans seem not to identify with any one single overriding problem as Americans. Though they know they're somehow different, many still cling to the idea that Mexican Americans are Caucasian, thus white, thus "one of the boys."

Many prove it: by looking and living like white Americans, by obtaining and keeping good jobs, and by intermarrying with Anglos who rarely think of it as a mixed marriage. To these people, Mexican Americans are assimilating well into white American society. They felt uncomfortable about the Commission's hearing because in their eyes it would merely tend to continue the polarization of Anglos and Mexican Americans at a time in which they felt it was disappearing.

To many other Mexican Americans, especially the young activists, Mexican Americans have for too long been cheated by tacitly agreeing to be Caucasian in name only. They say they would rather be proud of their Indian blood than uncertain about their Caucasian status. They feel they can achieve greater dignity by identifying with pre-Anglo Mexican Indian civilizations and even the Conquistadores than by pretending that they can truly relate to the *Mayflower* and early New England Puritanism.

This division of feeling will continue and perhaps widen. The hearing, however, clearly showed that people who are indigenous to the Southwest seem sometimes strangers in their own land and certainly in many ways curiously alienated from their fellow Americans.

ENRIQUE HANK LÓPEZ

Overkill at the Silver Dollar

Chicano response to the death of Rubén Salazar on that tumultuous August afternoon in 1970 was bitter. Some felt scalding anger, others merely accepted it as another in a continuing series of frustrating defeats. Among those who attended the funeral was Enrique Hank López, who came to the West Coast to pay his last respects to his slain friend. What happened to López, and how he interpreted it, is recorded in this article, which appeared in The Nation *magazine and was later reprinted in the East Los Angeles magazine* Con Safos. *Born and raised in a Denver barrio, López has a law degree from Harvard and is the author of numerous articles and several books.*

It was nearly midnight, and the barrio strangely quiet, quiet with fear. I had just left the Carioca restaurant with a dozen tortillas de maíz in a paper bag. I was spending the night before the funeral at my mother's house, and she'd promised to cook my favorite breakfast of menudo con chile. The tortillas, naturally, were essential.

Suddenly a police car screeched to a stop at the curb. Two cops jumped out and pushed me against the wall, frisking me from top to bottom with rough, insolent hands. They said not a word, and neither did I. I was simply not macho enough to protest. A cop like these had blasted the skull of my friend Rubén Salazar, the Chicano columnist for the *Los Angeles Times*, in the Silver Dollar Café, and I was frankly afraid to cross them.

They have also arrested about three hundred Chicanos since the police riot that erupted during the East Los Angeles peace rally that Rubén was covering on the afternoon he was killed. I didn't want to be prisoner 301 — and having flown all the way from New York, I certainly didn't want to miss Rubén's funeral. So I accepted the indignity of their frisk with a gut-souring meekness. This is all familiar stuff to anyone who has lived in a Chicano barrio. And when they yanked off my shoes and shook them upside-down, I clamped my mouth to hold back the sour saliva that I'd like to spit in their faces.

"What do you do?" one of them asked.

"I'm a lawyer and a writer."

"Oh — one of those guys."

Suddenly noticing the brown paper bag in my hand, one of these guardians of the peace grabbed it and quickly shuffled through the tortillas in an apparent search for marijuana or heroin. Finding none, he gave them back. Later on I threw the tortillas into a trash can — they must have had a hundred cop fingerprints on them.

They let me go finally — a tribute to my meekness, to what I would rather call my old barrio wisdom. The pragmatism of fear. And in my confusion and resentment (or was it again a sense of prudent resignation?) I had not noticed their badge numbers. Nor would I be able to recognize their faces again. I'm afraid all cops' faces have begun to look alike to me. And that's tragic, in a way, because two years ago I wrote to Mayor Lindsay and the New York Police Commissioner, commending a police officer who had been extremely kind (fatherly-kind) to my ten-year-old daughter when she was injured near our apartment while we were away, the babysitter having gone astray. He had taken her to a hospital and stayed by her side for five hours. So it's not in me to be a cop hater.

Just below Soto and Brooklyn Avenue, while searching vainly for a cab on those deserted streets, I saw a police helicopter swishing over me like a giant insect, its bright, harsh searchlights probing the dark alleys and back yards of the barrio.

I wondered then if the police regard us Mexican Americans as a community of barricaded criminals. The phrase came easily at that moment because that very afternoon the *Times* had quoted an expert as saying that the kind of missile that killed Rubén "should be used only against a barricaded criminal." Gene Pember, a consultant for the Peace Officers Standards and Training Commission, had told newsmen that the high-velocity tear-gas projectile that pierced Rubén's skull should never be used for crowd control, that "the thing is like a young cannon, really." Such missiles, he said, could go through a thick stucco wall. "That's what they are for — to penetrate a house or an object behind which a dangerous suspect has barricaded himself. But even then they should never be fired at a person."

The ten-inch missile that killed Salazar was fired by a sheriff's deputy *through an open doorway* at a point-blank range of fifteen feet. The deputy who fired that missile may not have known it was Rubén Salazar he was shooting, but he certainly knew it was a Chicano.

Yet, not once during the entire week following this obvious example of heedless slaughter would Sheriff Pitchess admit that his men might have been even slightly negligent. Sam Houston Johnson once told me that his brother LBJ suffered from a profound inability to say "I'm sorry" — to admit any error, however inconsequential. Certainly a tragic flaw in a human being, and I wonder if the Los Angeles sheriff shares that affliction. Far from blaming any of his men, he keeps talking about "outside agitators."

Small wonder that my fellow Chicanos are willing to believe almost any accusation against the police. When the *Times* subsequently devoted its entire front page to blown-up photos from a community newspaper called *La Raza*, quoting at length from an article titled "The Murder of Rubén Salazar" — they may have begun to entertain even that suspicion.

Earlier that evening (several hours before the cops frisked me) I had attended a rally of Chicanos at the All Nations Auditorium, where I heard their collective rage and frustration — my own as well — burst from the throats of one speaker after another, the packed listeners periodically stamping their feet and raising clenched fists as a symbol of "Chicano power." The speeches were mostly in

English but occasionally resorted to a schizolingual amalgam of English and Spanish to stress a vital point. Tough barrio language, most of it spoken with the bitterness of long years of resentment, some of it with a hushed, melancholy sense of bitter resignation.

When Corky Gonzales was introduced, a thunder of shoes stomped the floor and a chorus of "Viva Chicano power!" echoed from the walls, throbbing in my head, sending an expectant chill up my spine. But there was no flaming rhetoric from the much-loved leader of the Crusade for Justice — no call to arms, no threat of violence. There was instead an urgent plea for Chicano unity, for a grass-roots drive for political power, for a reclaiming of "the occupied territory of Aztlán" — that portion of the United States that once belonged to Mexico. It sounded more like a psychic take-back than a real one. The muted anger in his voice was spiced with humorous irony when he told the crowd, "I was busted at the peace rally and charged with suspicion of robbery because I had $325 in my billfold. To the gabacho[1] cops, I guess it's suspicious for a Chicano to have that much bread."

Clearly moved by Corky's mesmeric hold on the audience, René Anselmo (an Anglo millionaire who owns three TV stations) instantly donated one hundred dollars to the bail-bond fund for the three hundred Chicanos who had been arrested since the riot. By coincidence, Captain Ernest Medina — defendant in the My Lai massacre[2] case — was in Los Angeles during that same period, seeking donations for his defense from fellow Mexican Americans. I doubt that he could have raised two cents from the people who heard Corky, though I'm told that American Legionnaires in his hometown think him a hero.

After the rally I went to the Carioca bar-restaurant to eat Mexican food. It was also a sentimental gesture. The last time I had seen Rubén Salazar we had come to this

1 *gabacho* Anglo
2 *My Lai massacre* in the Vietnam War

restaurant, mostly to hear the mariachi trio that entertains here. They had played our favorite "Adelita" and "Siete Leguas," songs of the Mexican Revolution that led us into a pleasant nostalgic mood. I had once written that my father was the only private in Pancho Villa's army, and he was now claiming that *his* father was the only private, smiling in that gentle way he had, his eyes shining with impish enjoyment. What better basis for a deep and abiding friendship than our mutual conviction that *each* of our fathers was the only private in that famous rebel Division del Norte?

Our conversation became serious after a while. Rubén was deeply concerned about the laggard pace of bilingual education programs for Chicano children in the early grades. Most educators know that everyone's greatest, most intense period of learning is from birth to the age of five. For a Chicano that fast-paced, crucial learning is acquired in Spanish or in a pocho combination of Spanish and English. But the day he enters kindergarten — a day of intense anxiety even for a child from the most secure Anglo environment — that learning tool is snatched away. He's not permitted to speak the only language he knows. So he sits in frustration, confusion, and fright as the teacher and the "more advantaged" kids talk in alien sounds, making him feel dumb and lost. The experience is repeated hour after hour, day after day, until he's ultimately defeated. There is no one more fragile than a five-year-old child on alien turf.

The Chicano brings failure to school with him; he has no chance of success, no possibility of the "reward and reinforcement" that child educators feel is indispensable. The high school dropout rate for Mexican Americans (58 percent in some Chicano ghettos — higher than the rate for black students) is a belated symptom of the dropping out that begins on the first day of kindergarten.

"Why can't they teach our Chicano kids in both Spanish and English?" asked Rubén, fingering an empty glass. "If they could have genuine bilingual classes — Spanish in the morning and English in the afternoon — there would be some trace of comforting familiarity between school and their home. They could feel successful in Spanish, capable of learning. They wouldn't feel dumb, they wouldn't quit trying as they do now. With a gradual transition in kindergarten and the first two grades, English would be easier."

His convictions were an echo of educational theories developed by Dr. Jerome Bruner, director of Harvard's Center for Cognitive Studies, who has said that ghetto youngsters often face insuperable linguistic and environmental obstacles.

Ordering another round of margaritas that evening, we talked of other problems that bedevil Chicano kids. Thinking of the kid-glove treatment used on the Kennedy-Shriver cousins when they were arrested for possession of marijuana, we were both sure that a Chicano or black teenager would have been summarily convicted and sent to a reformatory for at least six months.

I told Rubén of my first encounter with the juvenile court system as a lawyer (I'd had several as a child). A Mexican American woman had called my office in a state verging on hysteria. Her thirteen-year-old son — let's call him Ramón Gómez — had been picked up by the police and whisked off in a squad car, but no one at the local precinct station would tell her where he was. Within half an hour we were at the Hollenbeck station in East Los Angeles and were informed that Ramón wasn't there. No record of his arrest. Then we hurried to the Juvenile Detention Home, where the desk captain said there was no booking on a Ramón Gómez. But as we were leaving, a young Chicano trusty told us that a boy answering Ramón's description had been taken from the detention home to the Los Angeles General Hospital. "He had a bloody bandage on his face." Checking the prison ward at the hospital, we learned two hours later that he'd received treatment for a fractured nose and then been returned to the detention home.

When we tried to see him at the so-called home, we were told he couldn't have visitors — nor could I see him in my capacity as his attorney. Angered by this refusal (any adult prisoner can see a lawyer), I went to a bail bondsman, who told me that kids weren't entitled to release on bail. Then I called several judges, who told me that they couldn't order his release on a writ of habeas corpus because children weren't entitled to that constitutional right.

When I finally saw the boy, he told me that he'd been accused of trying to break into a bubble-gum machine. "I put a penny in there and the gum didn't come out, so I was shaking it when the police came by. And when I tried to explain what happened, one of them slapped me. Then when I protested, they got me in the car, and one of them started punching my face with his closed fist, calling me a smart-aleck spic. That's how my nose got busted."

The Kafkaesque nightmare continued the next day at Ramón's hearing in juvenile court. The judge immediately informed me that I couldn't act as his lawyer "because this is not a criminal proceeding."

"Then why are you treating him like a criminal?" I asked. "Why has he been detained in that jail?"

"That's not a jail," he said rather testily. "It's only a detention home."

Paraphrasing Gertrude Stein, I said: "It has barred cells like a jail and barred gates to keep those kids inside, and a jail is a jail is a jail—no matter what name you give it."

But he still wouldn't let me appear as Ramón's lawyer, so his mother and I just sat there watching the nightmare proceedings of that quick-justice cafeteria called a "court." Not only were the juvenile defendants (almost all of them black or Chicano) denied lawyers; they couldn't face their accusers, they couldn't cross-examine witnesses against them, they couldn't object to rank hearsay testimony, they weren't protected by any of the normal rules of evidence. They were, in fact, unable to invoke any of the constitutional safeguards that are available to known gangsters.

And when I asked the judge for a transcript of the hearing after he had sentenced Ramón to six months in a reformatory, his mother pleaded with me not to appeal the case. "If we raise a big fuss," she said, "they'll only make it tougher on Ramón when he gets out. He'll be a marked man. We Chicanos don't have a chance."

Rubén had a film of tears in his eyes when I told him about Ramón. He said, "Think of all the other Ramóns who've been in the same bag."

Ramón Gómez must be twenty years old by now. He may have been one of the tight-mouthed militants in the angry crowd at the All Nations Auditorium on the night before Rubén's funeral, listening to one speaker comment on the tear-gassing of children at the peace rally, listening to the bitter irony in Corky Gonzales' voice. He's heard, as most Chicanos have, that Corky is a marked man, that the FBI probably shadows him from one state to another as he goes from campus to campus, from barrio to barrio, asking his brown brothers to join in common cause. Ramón knows from personal experience (as do too many Chicanos who have been brutalized by certain cops, by the juvenile court system, by those crime-breeding reformatories), knows with a sickening fear, that the police may some day crowd in on Corky, and that tragic violence may result.

But quite aside from his own not-likely-to-be-forgotten experience with the law, Ramón knows about inferior ghetto schools with indifferent teachers, about poor substandard housing, about high unemployment in the barrio, about radio and television shows that demean and insult his fellow paisanos. And he must be aware that local and federal government agencies largely ignore the plight of eight million invisible Mexican Americans. And he certainly knows that the television networks, national magazines, and news syndicates are generally deaf to the despairing voices of the barrio, although the more strident voices from black ghettos get ample notice.

Those same news media have been outraged by the alarming increase of cop killers — and it is well they should be, for any killing is abhorrent. But they should also know that the phrase is sometimes reversed in the ghetto — that Chicanos and blacks and poor whites often talk about killer cops with equal abhorrence.

Ramón and the rest of us Chicanos have been urged to

turn a deaf ear to the dangerous cry of the militant, to listen instead to the voices of reason, to the voices of the people like Rubén Salazar. And though I myself felt slightly less than reasonable when those two cops shoved me against the wall on a dark lonely street, I would certainly agree that our only hope is reason and good will.

One must also hope that the police and other authorities will come to realize that reason flows both ways, that this fragile society can ill afford the frightening consequences of the kind of overkill that silenced the most reasonable voice of Rubén Salazar.

ALURISTA

when raza?

The opening work in Alurista's Floricanto en Aztlán *collection, "when raza?" sounds a call to action. Anyone who has ever felt the impulse to do something, to make a decision, or to effect some kind of change can appreciate the sense of urgency which impels the author's words. A key word in the poem is* mañana — *which Alurista here gives a special significance.*

when raza?
when . . .
    yesterday's gone
and
    mañana
mañana doesn't come
    for he who waits
no morrow
    only for he who is now
to whom when equals now
he will see a morrow
mañana La Raza
    la gente que espera
no verá mañana[1]
our tomorrow es hoy
    ahorita
que VIVA LA RAZA
    mi gente[2]
our people to freedom
    when?
now, ahorita define tu mañana hoy[3]

1 *la gente . . . mañana* people who wait/will not see tomorrow. 2 *es hoy . . . mi gente* is today/this very moment/long live La Raza/my people. 3 *ahorita . . . hoy* this very moment define your tomorrow today

Index